How to get an A grade

OCR Philosophy & Ethics

Peter Baron

Published by Inducit Learning Ltd trading as pushmepress.com,

Pawlett House, West Street, Somerton,

Somerset TA11 7PS, United Kingdom

www.pushmepress.com

First published in 2013

ISBN: 978-1-909618-00-8

G571,572,581,582 specifications and past exam questions © OCR Examination Board, used with permission

All images © their respective owners

Links, reviews, news and revision materials available on

www.philosophicalinvestigations.co.uk

With over 20,000 visitors a month, the philosophical investigations website allows students and teachers to explore Philosophy of Religion and Ethics through handouts, film clips, presentations, case studies, extracts, games and academic articles.

Pitched just right, and so much more than a text book, here is a place to engage with critical reflection whatever your level. Marked student essays are also posted.

Contents

Introduction

I have spent most of my working life trying to get students A grades.

Of course, sometimes you don't succeed. But I have tried to encourage my students to apply these five principles, and I honestly believe that those who have done so have raised their chances considerably, and many have giving me a fantastic surprise, scoring way above my expectations.

But to do the analysis behind these five principles does take time - quite a lot of time, which I admit you may not have.

So in this book I've done it for you, using the OCR Philosophy and Ethics A level as my course. But you could apply the same steps to pretty much any exam board, and any subject, and if you do so, I think your prospects of A grade will be greatly enhanced.

- **PRINCIPLE 1** - Understand the philosophy behind your exam.

- **PRINCIPLE 2** - Do a close analysis of the exam syllabus.

- **PRINCIPLE 3** - Do a close analysis of past questions.

- **PRINCIPLE 4** - Do a close analysis of the relation between syllabus and questions.

- **PRINCIPLE 5** - Do a close analysis of the Chief Examiner's mark schemes and reports.

Finally, I include throughout the book some ideas on how to revise effectively, both as an individual and as a group, including a number of class revision exercises.

What are exams for?

Is there a reason for exams, a philosophy behind the subject you are doing?

The answer is yes, and it helps if you understand the philosophy behind Philosophy and Ethics, because in the end, if you become a philosopher and can show this in the exam, you should gain close to full marks.

The word philosophy means "a love of wisdom", and we gain wisdom by exercising a special type of thinking skill. The Greeks believed this skill was a foundational skill, because thinking well was a key to living well. So, we might ask, how do we "think well"?

I was encouraged recently to hear of a school which has a cookie club which meets at 4pm every week on a Thursday. The idea of the cookie club is to meet and debate - or if you like, to argue a case. Sometimes a member of staff, and sometimes a pupil comes with a case to defend, and everyone has to argue against the point of view that pupil is defending.

Something like this underlies the subject of philosophy. Philosophy is about presenting, arguing and then defending a case. So for example, *dn. law* Plato uses a method of dispute in his writing, called the Socratic method, where he puts words into the mouth of an adversary and then proceeds to dispute and disprove that opponent's case.

Of course this begs some questions.

WHAT DO I ACTUALLY BELIEVE ABOUT, SAY, GAY MARRIAGE?

I awarded a prize recently to anyone who could provide a good philosophical case against gay marriage. I announced the prize at a conference, and I guess it was no surprise that the speaker next to me murmured "there isn't one".

The speaker is of course wrong. The problem is, we sometimes need moral courage to oppose a view which most people hold. If I (for the sake of argument) oppose gay marriage, some people might call me a homophobe, other people may describe me as a right-wing fundamentalist, out of tune with reality.

But philosophers should not worry about this. Because philosophy is concerned with the nature and strength of arguments, and nothing else. People can cause me to take poison like Socrates had to, they can insult me in newspapers, and they can walk out of conferences. But we need to hold steadfastly to this point: social welfare only proceeds by the analysis and evaluation of arguments. It is only by this process that any great social reform has come. Bad arguments produce bad politics and bad policies and good arguments do the opposite.

In your A level, have the courage to present and then own for yourself, good, strong, well-justified arguments and you will be on the way to an A grade.

WHAT MAKES AN ARGUMENT WEAK?

A weak argument can really only be of two types. It can be logically unsound. And it can be factually unsound. Some arguments may present both weaknesses.

For example, consider this argument:

1. The world is either flat or square.

2. The world is not flat.

3. So the world must be square.

What is wrong with this? Well, it is false in two senses. First it commits a logical mistake - of restricting the options. It only gives us a choice of two possibilities, flat or square, when in fact there are many possible shapes, and the correct answer, the world is round, isn't given as a possibility.

Secondly, it is empirically or factually false. As a matter of fact, if I set off in my little sailing boat and head west (assuming I remember to navigate for the Panama Canal) I will eventually end up where I started. So I can attack the argument on two grounds, the logical and the factual, making clear what my two grounds are.

What about this argument about abortion:

1. The foetus resembles a human being at eleven weeks.

2. Human beings have feelings, thoughts, and desires.

3. Therefore a foetus has feelings, thoughts and desires at eleven weeks.

What is wrong with this argument? It actually begs a question, or perhaps begs two questions. Is resembling a human being enough to infer that something is a human being? After all, statues, dolls, and toy soldiers all resemble human beings. But that doesn't mean they are human beings.

Secondly, it lists a number of things that human beings do; they feel, think and want things. These may be necessary conditions for being human - it's hard to imagine a human being, except one in a persistent vegetative state, that doesn't at least have feelings. But is that list sufficient for defining a human being? After all my dog feels, thinks and wants its walk at 8am, but I wouldn't call my dog human.

Some facts are important for ethics. It is morally important where we can establish beyond doubt that the planet is warming. It is morally important whether a foetus feels pain, and at what stage of development. It is morally important in IVF treatment to know how many cycles a woman is allowed on the NHS and what the chances of success are - as these raise questions of rights and justice. Is it fair that my hospital excludes women over 37 from treatment? It is morally important to know who suffers when Trafigura dumps toxic waste in the Ivory Coast, and how much compensation the inhabitants deserve for their suffering.

But of course, we must check the facts. Bad facts produce bad ethics - and it wasn't long ago that some people were arguing that certain races were less intelligent than others, as a monstrous argument for discrimination, well considered in the recent film on President Lincoln.

WHAT MAKES AN ARGUMENT STRONG?

A strong argument proceeds by a logical form, from assumptions to conclusion. On the way the argument requires analysis and, if the question demands it, evaluation. Many students don't understand the difference between analysis and evaluation, so perhaps we can clarify this.

Analysis means that an argument proceeds by a process of reasoning. When we reason we substantiate (back up) the argument. This means we give justifications for a particular viewpoint. For example, we say that Kant argues that morality is an a priori process of reasoning, because he sees the moral ought as applying universally, everywhere, and for all time. If this is the case, then he argues we cannot be subject to the realm of emotions or peer group pressure, because this would make the moral ought conditional on what people think or feel at any particular time.

Notice that in this argument I use the word "because" a number of times. I spell out the reasons for my reasoning. I also use a hypothetical statement, which starts with if and then continues with then. The "if" here is indicating an underlying assumption, that we can divide the world up into two realms of thinking, what Kant calls the noumenal world (of pure ideas) and the phenomenal world (of experiences that we feel, see, touch).

If I was evaluating Kant rather than giving a Kantian analysis, then I might question this assumption. Is it a good way of looking at the world? Can there really be a pure realm of ideas in themselves? How does this differ from the utilitarian view of the world, and is the utilitarian view superior? If so, why? If not, why not?

But notice that if the examiner is asking me just to explain the Kantian worldview (as will happen at AS level in part a. of a question) then any evaluation is irrelevant. However, if we are asked to evaluate or even discuss Kant's worldview (as could happen at AS part b. of a question, or at A2 level, where in OCR we are still expected to know about Kant and apply him to sexual ethics, for example) then such a discussion is certainly relevant.

WHAT MAKES AN ARGUMENT INTERESTING?

Believe it or not the examiner can get bored reading the same textbook-regurgitated stuff script after script. So we need to make our arguments interesting. There are two main ways of doing this.

Make your argument different

For example, where most candidates might be expected to approve of utilitarian ethics (as it's the dominant way of thinking ethically in our society), why not attack utilitarian ethics? We could take as our starting point Arthur Koestler's quote, that people, in the name of utilitarianism, "have visited upon the human race such terrible privations..." and develop this idea. Our development might go like this: Governments claim to be arbiters of the common good. In imposing a decision on society, they can, for utilitarian reasons, ignore dissenters and the rights of those who are adversely affected. They can justify this in the name of progress and general welfare. Which is exactly what totalitarian governments have done. You could then connect this idea to Stalin's forced collectivisation which led to the deaths of over ten million Russians.

Make your examples real

Examiners like us to use examples which are up-to-date or personal. In order to do this, we could use a film to illustrate our argument. Imagine we are talking about virtue ethics. We could use the film Untouchable, which shows how an unemployed man caring for a disabled rich man in Paris would transform his life by relating to him as a human being with real needs and feelings, rather than as a category of "disabled". In this way the care worker shows that goodness isn't about rules (how I should care for people) but about character traits, things such as honesty, integrity, compassion and humour (which was one of Aristotle's key virtues).

Or we could take an example from our own experience. Should we ever save a stranger in distress? Has anyone ever saved you, or have you ever saved a stranger? What is the moral motivation for doing so? Is it a feeling (which seems to argue against Kant) or a sense of duty (which seems to argue for Kant's idea that we act on duty alone)?

Or we might use books we are reading, novels, biographies or everyday descriptions from books. The point is, make our essays interesting and show we can relate abstract ethics and philosophy to real life, and we will make an A grade much more likely. That's one way of producing A grade reflection.

HOW DO I PRACTISE STRENGTHENING ARGUMENTS?

I wrote a book last year with my colleague Brian Poxon called "How to Write Philosophy Essays". In that book we describe a technique for writing essays. Here's a brief description of how this technique works.

Imagine I have an essay title like "Miracles are unbelievable because they break natural laws", Discuss. I need to practise presenting what we can call my thesis in the first line of the essay. The thesis is simply your statement of your line of reasoning on this particular question. For example, my thesis might be "Miracles are believable because, although they may break natural laws, they do not have to do so; they may simply be unusual events, and even if they do break natural laws, they are miracles because they reflect who God is rather than human ideas of what is possible".

This statement has the advantages of being unmistakably relevant to this exact question and also very clear. The second thing I can do is reduce every paragraph to a one sentence statement of the argument of that paragraph.

- **THESIS** - Miracles are believable because they depend on God's character not on human ideas of scientific possibility.

- **PARAGRAPH 1** - The biologist Richard Dawkins argues that nothing is possible outside of a scientific probability which is determined by our understanding of natural laws.

- **PARAGRAPH 2** - Many events are outside scientific understanding. Give examples.

- **PARAGRAPH 3** - The miraculous can mean one of two things - the improbable or the impossible. Quote some other authors (eg

Swinburne).

- **PARAGRAPH 4** - The biblical account of miracles sees them as signs which point to the nature of God - as Creator (Jesus walks on water showing creator power), and redeemer (Jesus heals people with words like "Go in faith" and "Your sins are forgiven").

- **CONCLUSION** - Judging miracles by scientific criteria is misguided as miracles should be judged against the probability or otherwise of the existence of God.

So, try to sketch out a thesis, practise this technique, and then try saying something interesting, surprising even, which of course must be fully justified. This is how you maximise chances of an A grade.

WHY DO DEFINITIONS MATTER SO MUCH?

In Philosophy of Religion and Ethics there is technical vocabulary which must be used correctly. But we need to be aware that the task of philosophy is also to indicate ambiguities in key words, how they are used differently in different contexts and how the meaning is not necessarily clear-cut or fixed.

I was listening to a debate on Question Time recently and it became clear to me that two sides of this debate were actually talking about a different thing. The subject was gay marriage. On one side, the definition of marriage here meant something like "a relationship where two people are fully committed to one another". No mention of sexual relations here.

On the other side, the definition was something like this: "marriage is a lifelong commitment between a man and a woman where heterosexual sex is the natural expression, and children the natural fruit, of such a lifelong commitment". Notice that this definition includes both sex and the possibility of children.

I think the chairman of this debate, David Dimbleby, should have pointed out that people were talking about two different things. The question is, which is the correct definition, or the most useful definition? Clearly the second is the traditional view of marriage, whereby not having sexual relations is a ground for divorce or annulment of the marriage. Once we have established we are talking about different things we can then decide what we think.

Does it matter that the definition of marriage is changing? Should marriage necessarily include some idea of sexual relations if it doesn't, could I marry someone who remains my best friend, who I never even touch? If marriage includes some idea of sexual relations, how do we define sexual relations between two men?

All this helps to clarify the debate - and this is the task of philosophy. For philosophy has at its heart a philosophy of argument - of clarification, reasoning and conclusions which make sense. To argue effectively we cannot help defining and clarifying our terms, and indicating possible ambiguities in their use. The examiner's reports, analysed in the final chapter, repeatedly emphasise a failure to grasp key terms is a major reason why candidates don't get A grades.

How to Analyse the Specification

Students can sometimes be surprised by questions set in the exam. However, there never should be any element of surprise, as the specifications (syllabuses) lay down exactly what you can expect in the exam. Therefore surprise can only come because there is an area of the specification we failed to notice, or failed to cover adequately. A grade technique involves:

- Examining the specification, paying close attention to specific authors mentioned.

- Relating past questions to the specification to see how the examiner interprets the specification, which may be ambiguous in places.

In this section we will analyse the four specifications, before matching the specification to past questions in a later chapter.

AS ETHICS (OCR G572)

Candidates should be able to demonstrate knowledge and understanding of:

- the concepts of absolutist and relativist morality;

- what it means to call an ethical theory absolutist and objective;

- what it means to call an ethical theory relativist and subjective;

- the terms deontological and teleological.

Candidates should be able discuss critically these concepts and their strengths and weaknesses.

Ethical theories: Natural Law

Candidates should be able to demonstrate knowledge and understanding of:

- the origins of Aquinas' Natural Law in Aristotle's idea of purpose;

- Aquinas' ideas of purpose and perfection;

- the use of reason to discover Natural Law;

- the primary and secondary precepts.

Candidates should be able to discuss critically these views and their strengths and weaknesses.

Ethical theories: Kantian ethics

Candidates should be able to demonstrate knowledge and understanding of:

- the difference between the Categorical and the Hypothetical Imperatives;

- the various formulations of the Categorical Imperative;

- Kant's understanding of the universalisation of maxims;

- Kant's theory of duty;

- Kant's ideas of the moral law, good will and the summum bonum.

Candidates should be able to discuss critically these theories and their strengths and weaknesses.

Ethical theories: Utilitarianism

Candidates should be able to demonstrate knowledge and understanding of:

- the classical forms of Utilitarianism from Bentham and Mill;

- the principle of Utility;

- the differences between the Utilitarianism of Bentham and of Mill;

- the Hedonic Calculus, higher and lower pleasures, quantity v. quality, and Act and Rule Utilitarianism;

- the Preference Utilitarianism of Peter Singer.

Candidates should be able to discuss critically these issues and their strengths and weaknesses.

Ethical theories: Religious ethics

Religious ethics - a study of the ethics of the religion chosen by the candidate

Candidates should be able to demonstrate knowledge and understanding of:

- the main ethical principles of the religion studied and how the followers of the religion make ethical decisions;

- the ways in which religion and morality may seem to be linked or be seen as separate from each other;

- how far morality may be seen as dependent on God (Divine Command theory);

- how far religious ethics may be seen as absolutist or relativist;

- how ethical theories may be considered religious.

Candidates should be able to discuss critically these issues and their strengths and weaknesses.

Applied ethics

The ethical theories:

- Natural Law;

- Kantian Ethics;

- Utilitarianism;

- Religious Ethics.

as applied to the ethical topics below.

▸ Abortion: the right to a child

Candidates should be able to demonstrate knowledge and understanding of:

- the concept of the 'Sanctity of Life' and how it applies to abortion;

- the concept of personhood as applied to abortion;

- the right to life as applied to abortion and the rights of all those involved;

- the issues of infertility and the right to a child;

- the status of the embryo;

- whether a child is a gift or a right;

- the application and the different approaches of the ethical theories listed above to abortion and the right to a child.

Candidates should be able to discuss critically these issues and their strengths and weaknesses.

▸ Euthanasia

Candidates should be able to demonstrate knowledge and understanding of:

- the concept of the 'Sanctity of Life' and how it applies to euthanasia;

- the concept of the 'Quality of Life' and how it applies to euthanasia;

- the right to life as applied to euthanasia;

- the application and the different approaches of the ethical theories listed above to euthanasia.

Candidates should be able to discuss critically these issues and their strengths and weaknesses.

▸ Genetic engineering

Candidates should be able to demonstrate knowledge and understanding of:

- the ethical questions raised by the different types of genetic engineering to humans, animals and plants; human embryo research;

- the application and the different approaches of the ethical theories listed above to genetic engineering.

Candidates should be able to discuss critically these issues and their strengths and weaknesses.

▸ **War and peace**

Candidates should be able to demonstrate knowledge and understanding of:

- the principles of 'Just War' and its application;

- the theories of ethical and religious pacifism;

- the application and the different approaches of the ethical theories listed above to war and peace.

Candidates should be able to discuss critically these issues and their strengths and weaknesses.

Technical language in the syllabus

As we read through these specifications some general points seem to stand out. The first is that the specification helpfully breaks each topic up into subheadings. The second is that these subheadings contain specific technical language. The examiner has listed the technical language which, as a minimum, we are expected to use, and which we might expect to appear in the questions set.

So what is the technical language? You could take this opportunity to tick off the ones you can define easily without looking up.

Technical language at Ethics AS level includes:

- Absolute

- Relative

- Subjective

- Objective

- Deontological

- Teleological

- Natural Law

- Primary precepts

- Secondary precepts

- Categorical Imperative

- Hypothetical Imperative

- Duty

- Summum bonum

- Act Utiltarianism

- Rule utilitarianism

- Principle of utility

- Hedonic calculus

- Qualitative pleasures

- Preference utilitarianism

- Personhood (the embryo)

- Sanctity of Life

- Right to a child

- Quality of Life (euthanasia)

- Just War

- Ethical pacifism

- Religious pacifism

Now this is a minimum list - there are more technical terms we might want to use in an essay - but we should start with this list and make sure we understand exactly what these terms mean and indeed, what the alternative interpretations of their meanings might be. For example, the term sanctity of life has a different meaning to a Kantian than it does to a Roman Catholic. To a Kantian, it means "never treating a human being as just a means to an end, but always also as an end in themselves". Of course, this begs the question of whether the embryo should be classed as a human being. But to a Roman Catholic, sanctity of life means "designed and created by God with absolute value" which includes embryonic life, as life begins at conception.

In the past I can think of two examples of questions which surprised students, but really should not have done. The examiner has asked the part a. AS question "Explain Peter Singer's Preference Utilitarianism" which is dealt with very inadequately by textbooks and which teachers often gloss over altogether (for a more detailed treatment see my book on Teleological Ethics). The part b. asked us to consider whether Preference Utilitarianism was the best form. These questions are quite challenging, but not unfair or surprising.

Secondly, the examiner has asked us the question: "Distinguish between ethical and religious pacifism". This again is clearly specified in the syllabus, so should come as no surprise, and yet students were often ill-prepared for this question, failing to see that much Just War theory is coming from religious tradition (be it Catholic or Islamic), and so ethical pacifism is a different if related idea. Indeed the phrase "ethical pacifism" is ambiguous as surely religious pacifism is ethical pacifism of one sort? A good answer might consider this, whilst also going on to explain, for example, a Kantian approach to pacifism as contained in his Essay on Perpetual Peace, or the view of the atheist Bertrand Russell who became a conscientious objector to the first World War.

Authors mentioned

The following authors are mentioned, and although the syllabus makes clear you are not expected to read original sources, I believe the A grade candidate will want to read these authors for themselves. Extracts are available on the website. There are no specific authors mentioned for the applied ethics side of the specification: a good student will however draw up their own list of authors who address issues raised by the specification.

- Aquinas

- Aristotle

- Kant

- Bentham

- Mill

- Singer

Critical discussion

You will have noticed that the phrase "candidates should be able to discuss critically these issues and their strengths and weaknesses" occurs again and again. We need to be able to discuss the issues critically. What might this phrase mean?

Firstly, as I mentioned above, we need to understand how Kant, or Mill, or Singer or Aquinas arrive at their conclusions. As they move from analysis to conclusion do they make any moves which we might consider are errors? And what are their starting points or assumptions?

Before we go any further we need to be clear that in part a. AS questions we are never expected to evaluate - in other words, we will never be asked to assess critically Kant's Categorical Imperative, or Aquinas' idea of rational purpose. However we might be asked to "Explain the major weaknesses of Kant's ethical theory", which sounds like evaluation but is actually analysis.

I would suggest two ways of preparing for this aspect of the syllabus. When we look at each theory, it is important to ask what the starting point or assumptions are, and to do this, we need to understand the worldview which the philosopher is coming from. In the table below I summarise how assumptions and worldview interact in the major ethical theories which we encounter at AS and A2.

THEORY	ASSUMPTIONS	OBJECTIONS
Relativism	There is no universal truth.	May be empirically false
Natural law	Humans by nature do good	Humans by nature are selfish and do more evil than good
Kantian ethics	Reason is divided between the noumenal and phenomenal realms, and morality belongs to the noumenal.	Moral principles seem to be derived by many philosophers from the natural or empirical world eg by adding up happiness.
Utilitarianism - Bentham	Pleasure is the only good.	There seem to be other "goods" such as duty.
	We can measure pleasure.	We can't measure pleasure in hedons or anything else.
Divine Command	God's word is clear and unambiguous on practical issues.	Ancient texts were written from one cultural perspective which often does not address our culture directly.

Utilitarianism - Mill	There are higher and lower pleasures	This is a difficult distinction to make without sounding snobbish.
	Rules are needed to maximise utility	Rules imply universal application - so when can you break them?
Virtue ethics	A virtue is an agreed character trait. This trait comes from the rational purpose (telos) of human beings.	We cannot agree on whether things like courage are really a moral virtue. What about the kamikaze pilot?

Secondly, I think we should all draw up tables of strengths and weaknesses, at least for the ethical theories in question. This is the approach I take in the philosophicalinvestigations website where you can find examples of such tables under each section. Bu when you do this, make sure you link counteracting views with a philosopher and preferably, a quote from a philosopher. Learn some of these evaluative quotes for the exam, as they give you ideas which you can develop in the substance of your own essays. The extracts in each section (listed as Extract 1, Extract 2 etc) are also presented in each section on the website to help you extract key quotes and ideas from philosophers both dead and alive, so that your essays can gain more weight and a sense of engagement with ideas.

At A2 OCR the part a. and part b. format disappears, and so we expect to do the analysis and evaluation in one continuous thread of argument. Indeed this is the best approach, as the examiner has hinted that tagging evaluation on at the end weakens the essay.

A2 ETHICS (OCR G582)

Ethical topics and theories: Meta-ethics

Meta-ethics candidates should be able to demonstrate knowledge and understanding of:

- The use of ethical language - the ways in which different scholars understand how words like 'good', 'bad', 'right', 'wrong' are used when ethical statements are made.

- How meta-ethics differs from normative ethics.

- The different approaches: cognitive and non-cognitive; ethical naturalism, intuitionism; emotivism and prescriptivism and how these apply to ethical statements.

Candidates should be able to discuss these areas critically and their strengths and weaknesses.

Ethical topics and theories: Free will and determinism

Free will and determinism candidates should be able to demonstrate knowledge and understanding of:

- Hard determinism, soft determinism and libertarianism.

- The views of Darrow, Honderich, Hume and Locke.

- Theological determinism (predestination) and religious ideas of free will.

- The influences of genetics, psychology, environment or social conditioning on moral choices.

- The implications of these views for moral responsibility.

- The link between free will, determinism and moral responsibility.

Candidates should be able to discuss these areas critically and their strengths and weaknesses.

Ethical topics and theories: Nature and role of the conscience

The nature and role of the conscience Candidates should be able to demonstrate knowledge and understanding of:

- The different views of the conscience as God-given, innate or the voice of reason or instilled by society, parents, authority figures.

- Whether conscience is a reliable guide to ethical decision-making.

- The views of Augustine, Aquinas, Butler, Newman, Freud, Fromm, Piaget.

Candidates should be able to discuss these views critically and their strengths and weaknesses.

Ethical topics and theories: Virtue ethics

Virtue Ethics Candidates should be able to demonstrate knowledge and understanding of:

- The principles of Virtue Ethics from Aristotle.

- The 'agent-centred' nature of Virtue Ethics.

- The concepts of eudaimonia and the Golden Mean.

- The importance of practising the virtues and the example of virtuous people.

- More modern approaches to Virtue Ethics.

Candidates should be able to discuss these areas critically and their strengths and weaknesses.

Applied ethics

The ethical theories:

- Natural Law

- Kantian Ethics

- Utilitarianism

- Religious Ethics

- Virtue Ethics

as applied to all the applied ethics topics listed below.

Environmental and Business ethics

Candidates should be able to demonstrate knowledge and understanding of:

- The issue of how humans should relate to the environment, its resources and species

- Secular approaches - the Gaia hypothesis

- Issues in business ethics: the relationship between business and consumers; the relationship between employers and employees; the relationship between business and the environment; business and globalisation; the application and the different approaches of the ethical theories listed above to environmental and business ethics

Candidates should be able to discuss these areas critically.

Sexual ethics

Candidates should be able to demonstrate knowledge and understanding of:

- The issues surrounding sexual ethics - premarital and extramarital sex, contraception and homosexuality

- The application and the different approaches of the ethical theories listed above to sexual ethics

Candidates should be able to discuss these areas critically.

At A2 two areas have produced particular problems for students. The first is Meta-ethics or theories of ethical meaning. This produces difficulties because of the sheer weight of technical vocabulary (see list below). And it appears to be a little obscure why so many theories of the meaning of good are actually required.

But many philosophers would argue that meta-ethics is foundational to the subject as, remembering the discussion of the word marriage above, if we don't know exactly what we are talking about when we use the word "good" then we can find ourselves talking past one another. In fact today we live in an era of the resurgence of ethical naturalism, the view that ethical ideas have grounding in features of the natural world. This movement is led by philosophers like the virtue ethicist Alasdair MacIntyre, who wholeheartedly rejects the so-called naturalistic fallacy , and sees ethics grounded in a common idea of welfare derived from both the Bible and science.

The second area of difficulty comes with the introduction of environmental and business ethics into the syllabus. Teachers have been unsure how to handle this topic, and indeed, it does seem like two areas curiously conflated. Again, there is technical vocabulary to learn and some clarification to pursue as to how to use an idea like globalisation productively in an essay on ethics.

Technical vocabulary

Adopting the same approach we did at AS, it is best to list all the technical terms mentioned in the syllabus, and then make sure we have also noted all the specific authors mentioned so that we have something to say about each of them. The technical vocabulary relating to the ethical theories at AS still apply, as Natural law, Kant, Utilitarianism and Religious ethical theories will need to be applied to environment and business ethics and sexual ethics (the theory of virtue ethics is added to these theories at A2).

- Naturalism

- Cognitivism

- Non-cognitivism

- Prescriptivism

- Emotivism

- Intuitionism

- Hard determinism

- Soft determinism (compatibilism)

- Libertarianism

- Agent-centred virtue ethics

- Eudaimonia

- Golden Mean

- Gaia hypothesis

- Globalisation

- Extramarital sex

- Contraception

- Homosexuality

Again, it needs to be stressed that this is a minimum list of those terms mentioned specifically in the A2 syllabus. Past experience however suggests that these are the very terms which may appear in the exam question, and if they are not fully understood it will be impossible for candidates to answer these questions adequately. So learn them, understand them and know some of the possible variations of understanding of these terms. Major textbooks usually contain a glossary of key terms, but a word of warning: the way these definitions are reduced to one line means they lack nuance and may even be guilty of gross and misleading generalisations.

Authors mentioned

It is interesting just how many authors are specifically mentioned in the A2 ethics syllabus. This is important as the examiner may name one of them in the exam question and if you are underprepared on that one author you will be unable to do the question justice. So, again, I list them here for you to use as a checklist. I have listed these exactly in the order they come in the syllabus, so if you're in doubt which section a name refers to, then refer back to the syllabus.

- Darrow

- Honderich

- Hume

- Locke

- Augustine

- Aquinas

- Butler

- Newman

- Freud

- Fromm

- Piaget

- Aristotle

Again we need to stress this is a minimum list. For example, there are no philosophers mentioned in the Meta-ethics section of the syllabus so you will not be required to answer a question asking you to evaluate Alfred Ayer's view of goodness. But each of the theories mentioned, emotivism, prescriptivism, intuitionism have particular philosophers attached to them, so clearly underlying this section there are a number of names (Ayer, Hume, Hare, Moore, Ross, for instance).

Also, when we consider Virtue ethics, the examiner has made clear that answers simply dwelling on Aristotle (even though he is mentioned specifically in the syllabus) will not gain an A grade. So you or your teacher need to decide which of the modern virtue ethicists you intend to study in depth in order to fuflil that part of the syllabus asking us to consider modern virtue ethics (MacIntyre, Foot, Warnock, Slote, Louden for example).

Critical discussion

The A2 Ethics syllabus has left student and teacher with work to do filling in the gaps and interpreting how much additional content to supply. This comment particularly applies to three of the five sections: meta-ethics, virtue ethics and business and the environment.

However, we can be reasonably certain that the examiner wants us to contrast different views and then to decide, with justifications, which view we side with. This seems to be implicit in the command words "Discuss" or "Evaluate".

One way to prepare for the exam is to decide beforehand what your conclusion would be for any question the examiner might ask. For example, if we are asked to evaluate emotivism or prescriptivism or intuitionism it helps to have decided beforehand which theory we would side with, and why. What are the strengths and weaknesses of each? It is poor exam preparation to go into a paper unsure of your basic position.

So imagine we have the classic question "Goodness is merely an expression of personal feelings", Discuss. Underlying this question is the argument for or against emotivism. Suppose that we have decided that we quite like emotivism as a theory and thus wish to defend this assertion (whilst also considering objections to it of course).

I would then pre-prepare the following case: "Emotivism is the best explanation of the meaning of goodness because it recognises that the core element in statements of right and wrong is not reason, but feeling, and that no naturalistic explanation of the meaning of goodness escapes the naturalistic fallacy". I can then research some other authors, extract some quotes and make my own summary sheet around this base position - which could be adapted for another question such as "intuitionism is the best theory of the meaning of goodness", Discuss, which you could then disagree with using the same justification of emotivism as a counter-argument.

Similarly, when we consider Virtue Ethics, students are frequently unable to compare and contrast Aristotle and MacIntyre, the ancient and modern views of Virtue Ethics. How do they differ? In what ways do they agree? I need to prepare my basic position, whether I am to side with MacIntyre's version or Aristotle's. If I prefer Aristotle, I must be able and willing to defend the Greek world view that sees everything as having a purpose which is fulfilled according to some idea of perfection.

Finally, with environmental and business ethics it is probably fair to say that these two topics are just lumped together without much forethought as to how we should handle them. But that is no excuse for not mapping the territory clearly. Where there is inadequate structure in a syllabus, we must impose our own map to make sense of it. I do this on the website by drawing some diagrams elucidating the difference between ideas of intrinsic and instrumental goodness - as Gaia theory argues that the environment is intrinsically good (but what does that mean exactly?) whereas Utilitarian and Kantian ethics can only see the environment as instrumentally good - utilitarianism because there is one sole good, human happiness, or possibly the welfare of all sentient beings, and Kant only considers ethics from the standpoint of rational beings.

AS PHILOSOPHY OF RELIGION (OCR G571)

Ancient Greek influences on philosophy of religion

Candidates are expected to have a basic knowledge of the thinking of Plato and Aristotle; they will not be expected to have first-hand knowledge of the texts. They should be able to highlight the strengths and weaknesses in the thinking of Plato and Aristotle in the areas specified below.

Plato: The analogy of the cave

▸ **The Republic VII. 514A–521B**

Candidates should be able to demonstrate knowledge and understanding of what might be represented in the Analogy of the Cave by the following:

- The prisoners

- The shadows

- The cave itself

- The outside world

- The sun

- The journey out of the cave and the return to the prisoners.

Candidates should be able to discuss critically the validity of the points being made in this analogy.

▸ Plato: The concept of the forms; the form of the good

Candidates should understand what Plato meant by 'Forms' and be able to demonstrate knowledge and understanding of:

- The relation between concepts and phenomena

- The concept of 'Ideals'

- The relation between the Form of the Good and the other Forms.

Candidates should be able to discuss critically the validity of the above points.

Aristotle: Ideas about cause and purpose in relation to God (metaphysics book 12)

Candidates should be able to demonstrate knowledge and understanding of:

- Aristotle's understanding of material, efficient, formal and final cause

- Aristotle's concept of the Prime Mover

Candidates should be able to discuss critically the validity of the above points.

Judaeo-Christian influences on philosophy of religion

Candidates should be familiar with Biblical texts to exemplify the topics below. There are no prescribed texts.

▸ The concept of God as creator

Candidates should be able to demonstrate knowledge and understanding of:

- The way the Bible presents God as involved with his creation

- The imagery of God as a craftsman

- The concepts of omnipotence, omniscience and omnipresence

- The concept of 'creatio ex nihilo'

Candidates should be able to:

- Compare this view with Aristotle's Prime Mover

- Discuss whether, if God created the universe, God is therefore responsible for everything that happens in it

Candidates should be able to discuss these areas in a critical manner.

▸ The goodness of God

Candidates should be able to demonstrate knowledge and understanding of:

- The ways in which the God of the Bible is seen as morally perfect and the source of human ethics

- The concept of God as lawgiver and as judge

Candidates should be able to:

- Consider whether, in a Biblical context, God commands things because they are good or whether things are good because God commands them

Candidates should be able to discuss these areas in a critical manner.

‣ Traditional arguments for the existence of God

The Ontological argument from Anselm and Descartes; challenges from Gaunilo and Kant.

Candidates should be able to demonstrate knowledge and understanding of:

- The Ontological argument from Anselm and Descartes

- Challenges to it from Gaunilo and Kant

- Anselm's understanding of God – his understanding of the differences between contingent and necessary existence

- Descartes' understanding of existence as a perfection which God cannot lack

- Gaunilo's analogy of the island in On Behalf of the Fool

Candidates should be able to discuss these areas in a critical manner.

▸ The cosmological argument from Aquinas and Copleston; challenges from Hume and Russell

Candidates should be able to demonstrate knowledge and understanding of:

- The Cosmological argument from Aquinas and Copleston

- The arguments put forward by Copleston in the 1948 radio debate with Russell and Russell's counter arguments

- Hume's criticisms of the cosmological argument

Candidates should be able to discuss critically these views and their strengths and weaknesses.

▸ The teleological argument from Aquinas and Paley; challenges from Hume, Mill and Darwin

Candidates should be able to demonstrate knowledge and understanding of:

- The teleological argument from Aquinas and Paley

- The challenges to it from Hume, Mill and Darwinism

Candidates should be able to discuss critically these views and their strengths and weaknesses.

▸ **The moral argument from Kant: psychological challenges from Freud**

- The moral argument from Kant, including his concept of the 'summum bonum' and his inferences about innate moral awareness

- Psychological challenges from Freud to the moral argument, his view that moral awareness comes from sources other than God

Candidates should be able to discuss critically these views and their strengths and weaknesses.

Challenges to religious belief

▸ **The problem of evil**

Candidates should be able to demonstrate knowledge and understanding of:

- The problem of evil: the classic theodicies of Augustine and Irenaeus

- The nature of the problem of evil and the possible differences between natural and moral evil

- How each theodicy understands the responsibility of God for the existence of evil in the world

- The origins of evil and the role of human free will

Candidates should be able to discuss critically these approaches and their strengths and weaknesses.

▸ Religion and science

Candidates should be able to demonstrate knowledge and understanding of:

- Scientific and philosophical views on the creation of the universe; particularly the debate between Creationism and the Big Bang theory

- Darwinism and various developments of evolutionary theory

- 'Intelligent Design' and 'Irreducible Complexity'

- Religious responses to challenges posed by scientific views

Candidates should be able to discuss critically these views and their strengths and weaknesses.

Technical language in the syllabus

The following phrases or technical terms occur in the syllabus (in order of appearance below). They represent a minimum checklist of technical vocabulary. These terms, and only these terms, may appear in an exam question, and so you will be hampered in your answer if you don't understand how they are used (and any ambiguity or difference in use by philosophers).

- The Form of the Good

- Ideals

- Phenomena

- Material, Efficient, Formal and Final Cause

- Prime Mover

- Omnipotence

- Omniscience

- Omnipresence

- Creatio ex nihilo

- Cosmological argument

- Teleological argument

- Moral argument

- Summum bonum

- Theodicy

- Creationism

- Big Bang Theory

- Intelligent design

- Irreducible complexity

Authors mentioned

The following authors are listed in the syllabus, and so they should be carefully studied, with summary sheets of their views produced (the area of the syllabus to which each relates can be cross-referenced above). Also note that the need to critically consider these views means that some countervailing view also needs to be assessed. To do this you will need to specify some authors who do not agree with the views cited by the above. To find out these views first hand, consult the "extracts" section of the philosophicalinvestigations website, listed by syllabus heading.

- Plato (analogy of the Cave)

- Aristotle (Metaphysics book 12)

- Anselm (Ontological argument)

- Descartes

- Gaunilo

- Kant (criticisms of the Ontological argument)

- Aquinas (Cosmological argument)

- Copleston

- Russell (radio debate with Copleston)

- Hume (criticisms of cosmological argument)

- Aquinas (second appearance, this time the Teleological argument)

- Paley

- Hume (criticisms of teleological argument)

- Mill (criticisms)

- Darwin

- Kant (second appearance, this time the moral argument)

- Freud (psychological challenges)

- Augustine (free will)

- Irenaeus

- Darwin (religion and science debate)

The first thing we can note from this list is that there are twenty authors whose arguments we need to clarify. There is clearly potential for confusion here, and a good student needs to think carefully about the differences between these various arguments. Then there are additional authors that need to be added, for example, Richard Dawkins is not on the syllabus as a named author, but as a contemporary exponent of evolutionary design, he will need to be studied (and perhaps a good student will study him alongside Darwin to see how he developed Darwin's insights, with the theory of memes and the origin of conscience through the altruistic or "selfish gene" - which are actually the same thing, paradoxically, as it is the self-promoting gene which produces the requirement to co-operate together, and so produces over time the genetic basis for altruism or sense of sympathy and compassion for others).

There are also a number of texts which need to be studied. It is worth reading them for yourself, even though the syllabus states "the candidate will not be expected to have first-hand knowledge of the texts themselves", because the best way to gain full understanding is always to return to the original source and then compare that with what commentators say. Aristotle's Metaphysics 12 is mentioned as is Plato's Cave Analogy (Book VII, The Republic). The radio debate between Copleston and Russell needs to be studied carefully. Who do you think won it by producing the strongest argument for or against the cosmological argument? Be aware too that many of these arguments may be a number of different arguments - for example, Anselm produced at least two versions of the ontological argument for God's existence.

Ambiguities in the syllabus

In this syllabus there are a number of places where teacher and student have to fill in the gaps. A diligent student needs to keep an eye on these gaps: it is too easy for a teacher to run out of time and leave a gap unfilled. The difference between the A grade student and a lesser grade student is often that the A grade student is not too teacher dependent, but takes responsibility for their own understanding and interpretation of the syllabus, so making sure any gaps are filled whether they are covered in class or not.

Here's my list of gaps that need to be filled:

> "Biblical texts on the concept of God as creator and the goodness of God".

There are no set texts, meaning passages from the Bible, so we need to find some.

> "Consider whether, in a Biblical context, God commands things because they are good or whether things are good because God commands them".

This is a statement of "Euthyphro's dilemma" first argued by Plato in a fictitious discussion between Euthyphro and Socrates. You could look at the ten commandments for example, and see how these are given in the context of a revelation of the character of God (Exodus 20-34). Some would argue that the dilemma is itself a fallacy because it restricts the options to two: morality comes from God's words (commands) or from reason, whereas it could be argued int he context of Exodus 34 that the ten commandments are given because God is revealed as the "God of steadfast love and faithfulness" - there is a difference, by analogy, between a parent saying "do this because I say so" (command), and "do this because I love you and want the best for you". But this third option isn't considered by Euthyphro's dilemma, and so it closes off the most plausible biblical reason for the commands of God.

"The origins of evil" (Problem of Evil section)

This is a huge area of controversy which could embrace psychological theories such as behaviourism suggests, that we are conditioned by our environment to behave "evilly", to psychological theories of the origin of action in childhood (Freud, Piaget), to genetic influences. Because it is open-ended it is up to you to take whatever line you like on the issue of where evil comes from, but to ground your views in scholarship, and find your own authors to add to the above list.

You can continue this analysis of ambiguities for yourself: the important point is that every A grade student should do a close analysis of the syllabus and then continue to refer back and use the syllabus as your starting point. Many of these sections have sufficient leeway to make the statement "are we departing from the syllabus" (which I have heard teachers use) a fairly meaningless one. To some extent the syllabus is determined by you: and how you relate interconnected ideas to the main themes outlined above.

A2 PHILOSOPHY OF RELIGION (OCR G581)

Although the A2 syllabus appears on the face of it to be shorter, it includes some complex terminology and a series of quite challenging philosophical ideas. So again, a careful analysis of technical vocabulary, authors mentioned and ambiguities will help us clarify what is required of the A grade student.

Religious Language

Candidates should be able to demonstrate knowledge and understanding of:

- Religious language – uses and purpose

- the via negativa (Apophatic way)

- The verification and falsification principles

- Different views on the meaningfulness of religious language

- The uses of symbol, analogy and myth to express human understanding of God

- The views of the Vienna Circle, A. J. Ayer, Anthony Flew, Ludwig Wittgenstein and Paul Tillich on religious language

Candidates should be able to discuss these areas critically and their strengths and weaknesses.

Religious Experience

Candidates should be able to demonstrate knowledge and understanding of the following in relation to God and religious belief:

- Arguments from religious experience from William James

- The aims and main conclusions drawn by William James in The Varieties of Religious Experience

- The following different forms of religious experience:

  - Visions

  - Voices

  - 'Numinous' experience

  - Conversion experience

  - Corporate religious experience;

- The concept of revelation through sacred writings.

Candidates should be able to discuss these areas critically and their strengths and weaknesses.

Miracle

A study of how God might interact with humanity, by looking at the concept of miracle.

Candidates should be able to demonstrate knowledge and understanding of:

- Different definitions of miracle, including an understanding of Hume

- The biblical concept of miracle and the issues this raises about God's activity in the world

- The concept of miracle, and criticisms made by Hume and Wiles

- The implications of the concept of miracle for the problem of evil

Candidates should be able to discuss whether modern people can be expected to believe in miracles, and whether miracles suggest an arbitrary or partisan God. Candidates should be able to discuss these areas critically and their strengths and weaknesses.

Attributes

‣ Nature of God

Candidates should be able to demonstrate knowledge and understanding of:

- God as eternal, omniscient, omnipotent and omni-benevolent – and the philosophical problems arising from these concepts

- The views of Boethius in his discussion of eternity and God's foreknowledge in Book 5 of The Consolations of Philosophy

- The question as to whether or not a good God should reward and punish.

Candidates should be able to discuss these areas critically and their strengths and weaknesses.

Life and Death; The Soul

‣ Life and Death

Candidates should be able to demonstrate knowledge and understanding of:

- Distinctions between body and soul, as expressed in the thinking of Plato, Aristotle, John Hick and Richard Dawkins

- Other concepts of the body/soul distinction

- Different views of life after death: resurrection and reincarnation

- Questions surrounding the nature of disembodied existence

- The relationship between the afterlife and the problem of evil

Candidates should be able to discuss these areas critically and their strengths and weaknesses.

Technical Language in the syllabus

- Via negativa

- Apophatic way

- Verification principle

- Falsification principle

- Symbol

- Analogy

- Myth

- Numinous religious experience

- Corporate religious experience

- Miracle

- Omnipotent

- Omniscient

- Omni-benevolent

- Foreknowledge

- Soul

- Resurrection

- Reincarnation

Again we need to stress this is a minimum list - but represents terms which could appear in the actual exam question, and for this reason they must be throughly learned and understood. A good technique for an opening paragraph is to clarify and define your terms, making sure you indicate ambiguities within them. For example, many students assume the term "resurrection" is clear from the biblical accounts. But this is far from the case. Jesus appears as a physical body and yet he walks through closed doors and isn't recognised by his followers on the road to Emmaus. St Paul says we are "raised imperishable" with a "spiritual body" (1 Corinthians 15), but what does he mean by a "spiritual body"? Is it a replica of our old body, and if so, our old body at what state of existence (I wouldn't want to live eternally with a decrepit athritic body)? If it's not an exact replica, how is the resurrection body different? Simply outlining some of these difficulties allows us to proceed in an A grade direction.

Authors mentioned

- AJ Ayer

- Anthony Flew

- Ludwig Wittgenstein

- Paul Tillich

- William James (Varieties of Religious Experience)

- David Hume

- Maurice Wiles

- Boethius (Consolations of Philosophy Book V)

- Plato (Life after Death)

- Aristotle

- John Hick

- Richard Dawkins

There are twelve authors specifically mentioned and one key text (Boethius). However, there are a number of authors a good student would be unwise to neglect. For example, Richard Swinburne has written extensively on a number of issues here, not least life after death. Anthony Flew has written not just on religious language (where he is mentioned and so could appear in an actual question), but also on miracles and life after death. I would always encourage students to read some original sources and to quote the authors themselves. Many of these are on the philosophicalinvestigations website as extracts (go to each section and then scroll down to Extract 1, Extract 2, Extract 3 etc).

Ambiguities

There are always gaps to fill and interpretations to make of any syllabus. Here's a short list of the ones in the A2 Philosophy of Religion syllabus.

"Religious language - uses and purpose".

What exactly are the "uses" of religious language (worship, prayer, private meditation, parables, credal statements?).

"The concept of revelation through sacred writings".

The syllabus deliberately leaves this ambiguous because we can choose any religion to illustrate the idea of revelation, and different religions of the world take very different views on this. Assuming for the moment that we take Christianity as our religion, there are a number of different views of the status of the Bible. For example, you might read the Chicago statement on Biblical Inerrancy to find a contemporary justification for taking the Bible as the inerrant Word of God: the statement was written by American academics as recently as 1967. This could then be contrasted with liberal views of revelation, using insights from the religious language section (about how myth works for example). Many candidates fail to discuss non-propositional forms of revelation.

"The biblical concept of miracle".

Again, there is a central ambiguity here, not clarified by the syllabus. What is the biblical concept of miracle? Theologians take different views on this. What does seem true, however, is that the Bible doesn't take the definition of miracle which philosophers do. Philosophers tend to take a scientific view of miracle, as "an event which breaks natural law", whereas theologians tend to argue from the perspective of John's Gospel, that miracles are signs which tell us something about the nature of the Messiah (in the New Testament) or Yahweh (in the Hebrew Scriptures). These two ideas are sufficiently different to suggest that the term itself is ambiguous, and needs to be clarified against the worldview of two thousand years ago.

"Whether or not a good God should reward or punish".

This begs the question whether goodness includes some idea of justice (and a complete intolerance of sin inherent in the idea of holiness). The ideas of "reward" and "punishment" are also in need of careful treatment. Compare for example the idea of those who fail to attend to the needs of the poor in Matthew 25 "as if serving Christ himself" as the basis of judgement and casting into eternal fire, with the idea in John's gospel that "who believes in the Son has life, but he who does not believe has not life, and the wrath of God rests upon him". This seems to suggest that we are justified by belief (the Evangelical Protestant view that we are justified by faith alone) and punished accordingly. This appears to contradict the idea in Matthew 25, the parable of the Sheep and the Goats, that the basis of punishment is our actions on earth and whether we care for those less fortunate than ourselves in an appropriate way.

"Resurrection and reincarnation".

Here are two "big ideas". Unfortunately both are ambiguous. The idea of reincarnation operates differently in the Buddhist system of thought (and maybe in varieties of Buddhist thinking) than in Hindu thinking. Buddhists refer to "no-self" rather than different stages of reincarnated being (as in Hinduism). Thus the ambiguity of the term needs to be carefully addressed and critically evaluated. An A grade candidate will never assume we (or the syllabus itself) knows what we are talking about, especially when what we are talking about, once defined, so determines the nature of our analysis.

How to Analyse Past Exam Questions

Past exam questions give us critical clues as to how the examiner interprets the specification. As indicated in the previous chapter, the specification is ambiguous in several areas, and open to interpretation. What is certain is that no technical terms or authors will be mentioned in an exam question which isn't already mentioned in the syllabus.

The best approach to maximising A grade potential is to study carefully the trends in the questions, to examine which have been set before, and then relate them to the syllabus. Any areas that have never been examined before, or not for some time, are more likely to occur in the next paper set, as examiners have to range their questions across the whole syllabus and not stick to areas that may be easier to set questions on.

Over the page is a table giving all AS Ethics questions since 2010.

Note: The exact questions for June 2012 and January 2013 papers are still restricted by the exam board - for ten months after the exam. I have indicated the broad topic area by a cross. You should refer to the philosophicalinvestigations.co.uk website for exact wording - as soon as permitted, I will post them. Some crosses appear twice because questions may have an applied issue and a theory mentioned in the same question.

AS PHILOSOPHY OF RELIGION (OCR G571)

At AS level the questions are presented in two parts, part a. being worth 25 marks and part b. 10 marks. The marks roughly translate to the number of minutes you have to spend on each. So it is essential to practise in class time writing essays, first of all with some sort of plan, and then using memory alone.

The two parts also relate to different skills. There is no point wasting time in part a. questions evaluating the plausibility of some theory or view when the question title only ever asks you to explain some theory or viewpoint, or on occasions, to compare two viewpoints. The idea of comparison here involves lining two things up against each other, as you might compare two cars and observe differences between them: it does not mean you state a view of which view is superior to the other. This would be an evaluation skill and you are never required to evaluate at part a of a question, and so you will simply lose time if you do, and gain no credit.

- **REVISION TIP** - Read through each other's work and be ruthless about underlining in red any deviation from the question set, and any use of evaluative language in part a. questions. This will help you to really understand the difference between analysis and evaluation, and between comparing and critically comparing.

Note: The exact questions for June 2012 and January 2013 papers are still restricted by the exam board - for ten months after the exam. I have indicated the broad topic area by a cross. You should refer to the philosophicalinvestigations.co.uk website for exact wording - as soon as permitted, I will post them. Some crosses appear twice because questions may have an applied issue and a theory mentioned in the same question.

OCR G571	Plato/Aristotle	God of Classical Theism	Cosmological argument	Teleological argument	Moral argument	Ontological argument	Problem of evil	Science and religion
Jan 2010	a. Explain the concept of Ideals in Plato's writing. b. "Ideals are an illusion; we can only experience what is real". Discuss	a. Explain the concept of creatio ex nihilo. b. 'Nothing comes from nothing'. Discuss		a. Explain Mill's challenge to the teleological argument. b. Evaluate the claim that the universe has too many flaws for it to be designed				a. Explain Darwinism and evolutionary theory. b. 'The universe is too complex for evolutionary theory to explain it'. Discuss
June 2010		a. Compare the concept of Prime Mover with that of God as a craftsman. b. 'Utilitarianism can lead to wrong moral decisions.' Discuss.			a. Explain Freud's view that moral awareness comes from sources other than God. b. 'War should not be allowed even as a last resort'. Discuss	a. Explain Anselm's ontological argument. b. 'It is pointless to deny the logical necessity of the existence of God'. Discuss		
Jan 2011		a. Explain what it means to say God is good. b. To what extent are things only good because God commands them?		a. Explain Paley's argument for the existence of God. b. 'The universe has no purpose'. Discuss	a. Explain what Kant means by 'summum bonum'. b. 'The existence of morality is not evidence for the existence of God'. Discuss	a. Explain Anselm's ontological argument. b. 'There is no evidence of intelligent design in the universe'. Discuss	a. Explain why some creationists do not believe in the big bang theory. b. 'Scientists are the only ones who can explain why the universe is here'. Discuss	
June 2011	a. Explain Aristotle's understanding of the four causes. b. 'Aristotle's four causes fail as a description of the real world'. Discuss		a. Explain Hume's criticisms of the cosmological argument. b. To what extent was Hume successful in his criticisms of the cosmological argument				a. Explain the nature of evil. b. 'Moral evil may be the fault of humanity but moral evil is God's fault'. Discuss	
Jan 2012	a. Explain Aristotle's four causes. b. 'The Bible is too inconsistent to be used for moral teachings.' Discuss	a. Explain Biblical beliefs about the attributes of God. b. 'The Bible is too inconsistent to be used for moral teachings.' Discuss	a. Explain the arguments put forward in the Copleston in his radio debate with Russell. b. How far was Russell successful in countering Copleston's arguments in the radio debate.			a. Explain how Kant challenged the ontological argument. b. To what extent was Kant successful in his challenge to the ontological argument?	a. Explain the Irenaean theodicy. b. To what extent can evil be said simply to be a test?	a. Compare scientific and philosophical views on the creation of the universe. b. Evaluate the view that science can only explain how and not why the universe exists.
May 2012	a. X b. X	a. X b. X		a. X b. X	a. X b. X	a. X b. X	a. X b. X	a. X b. X
Jan 2013	a. X b. X	a. X b. X		a. X b. X	a. X b. X	a. X b. X	a. X b. X	a. X b. X

Spot the gaps

With eight topic areas there are sometimes up to three gaps before the examiner chooses to set a question again on a particular area. It is important also to look at possible questions that have not yet been set on a particular area. This is the subject of the next chapter.

Wording of the questions

The wording of part a. questions only contains two command words: "explain" and "compare". Notice that in part a. questions you will only be asked to explain rather than evaluate. So, again, we need to pay close attention to the specification and try putting the word "explain" in front of each subsection of the specification, or if there are two elements within an area of the specification, to compare them.

Which areas might we be expected to compare (a command word only used twice in essay titles since 2009)?

- Science v religion on the origins of the universe (Jan 2012)

- Prime Mover v God as craftsman (Jan 2010)

- Aristotle's Prime Mover v God as Creator ex nihilo

- Descartes' and Anselm's versions of the Ontological Argument

- Copleston's and Russell's view of the Cosmological Argument

- Kant's and Freud's view of the origin of moral awareness

- The theodicy of Iranaeus and Augustine

- **REVISION TIP** - try making up tables to compare these different views. The table could have sub-categories down the left hand side eg on science v religion. The subcategories might be: explanation, issues arising, problems/ weaknesses with the view, strengths of the view. An issue here might be whether the two views, of science and religion for example on creation can be reconciled, or the fact that there are a variety of religious views which need to be considered.

Part b questions

These ask you to evaluate a particular viewpoint. Most part b questions are statement followed by "discuss". There is no substitute for practising writing an answer in 10 minutes, which leaves time only for two or three paragraphs. It is important to launch straight into your answer and to work out before you start writing what your thesis (your argument in one line) is going to be. This will require the skill of clear thinking and writing if you are going to obtain the full ten marks in part b.

In your discussion remember to unpack the key word or words in the statement you are asked to discuss. For example, if we are asked to evaluate whether Kant is successful in his criticisms of the ontological argument (Jan 2012), we need to unpack what "successful" means here. And if we are asked to consider whether the Bible is too "inconsistent" (Jan 2012) we need to discuss what this word consistent might mean, and whether the concept of consistency is appropriate for a mythological Biblical worldview which produces a developing theology of God over 2,500 years and 66 books which make up the Old and New Testaments.

- **REVISION TIP** - Part b. questions, worth ten marks each, express an issue underlying that section of the syllabus. For example, with Plato's idea of the Forms, the issue is whether this is an adequate view of reality, whether reality is beyond human understanding or just reducible to what we observe. So practise making up your own part b. questions, as statement with the word "Discuss" after it, which go to the heart of the issues philosophers are debating on the different syllabus areas.

- **REVISION TIP** The examiner repeatedly stresses that candidates spend too long on part b. questions (worth only 10/35 marks) and not long enough on part a. questions (worth 25/35). You must practise explaining more fully (and reflectively, really going to the heart of what key ideas mean and where they come from) in part a, and evaluating succinctly in part b.

AS ETHICS (OCR G572)

Categories

The following questions follow the syllabus areas. Notice that some questions, particularly those containing an application to one of the issues listed (abortion, euthanasia, war and peace or genetic engineering) cross over two columns. For example, one part a. question from Mat 2011 reads "explain theories of ethical and religious pacifism". This crosses over the theoretical aspect of religious ethics and the theories of war and peace. In fact Just War theory comes out of the religious tradition, hence the overlap.

However, not all applied ethics questions have a mention of an ethical theory or theories. Two part a. questions from May 2012 simply state "Explain the issues surrounding euthanasia/right to a child". The expectation here is that the student mentions at least one or two of the theories studied, but the question itself gives no requirement as to which theories. You would be unwise just to mention issues such as sanctity of life, quality of life, individual rights (to name some issues surrounding euthanasia) without relating them to ethical theories. A word of warning though: the examiner comments in the report on this question "Many candidates used ethical theories to draw out moral issues and some were very successful in doing so, however, this approach to the question often meant that candidates missed the moral issues surrounding the right to a child and instead gave a general explanation of how the theories might approach the issue". It would be easy to fall into the trap of giving a simple GCSE style answer to this question which lacks depth or theoretical grounding, yet it is also easy to fall into the trap of answering a different question.

OCR G572	Absolute/relative	Utilitarianism	Natural Law	Kant	Religious Ethics	Abortion	Euthanasia	Just War	Right to a child	Genetic Engineering
Jan 2010	a. Explain what is meant by moral absolutism. b. "Moral absolutism cannot be justified". Discuss	a. Explain how utilitarians approach the issues of war. b. "Pacifism does more harm than good". Discuss	a. Explain the strengths of Natural Law Theory. b. To what extent could a follower of natural law accept embryo research?	a. Explain the strengths of Natural Law Theory	a. Explain how the ethics of a religion you have studied might be applied to abortion. b. "Religious ethics fail to consider consequences". Discuss	See religious ethics question a.		See utilitarianism questions a. & b.	See Natural law question b.	
June 2010	a. Explain the differences between absolute and relative morality. b. "Relativist theories give no convincing reasons why people should be good". Discuss	a. Explain the main strengths of Mill's Utilitarianism. b. "Utilitarianism can lead to wrong moral decisions". Discuss		a. Explain how the follower of Kantian ethics might approach the issues surrounding the right to a child. b. "The right to a child is an absolute right". Discuss	a. Explain the ethical principles of a religion you have studied in relation to war. b. "War should not be allowed even as a last resort". Discuss			See religious ethics questions a. & b.	See Kantian questions a. & b.	
Jan 2011	a. Explain how a moral relativist might approach issues raised by abortion. b. "A relativist approach to issues raised by abortion leads to wrong moral decisions". Discuss	a. Explain the difference between Act and Rule Utilitarianism. b. To what extent is Utilitarianism a useful method of making decisions about euthanasia?		a. Explain Kant's argument for using the Categorical Imperative. b. "The universalisation of maxims by Kant cannot be defended". Discuss	a. Explain how the followers of the ethics of a religion you have studied make ethical decisions. b. "Morality and religion are separate". Discuss	See relativism questions a. & b.	See Utilitarianism question part b.			

	Preference Utilitarianism / Bentham & Mill	Natural Law	Kant / Hypothetical & Categorical Imperative	War	Genetic engineering / Religious ethics	Personhood / Abortion	Pacifism / Killing	
May 2011	a. Explain the Preference Utilitarianism of Peter Singer b. To what extent is Preference Utilitarianism the best form of Utilitarianism?	a. Explain how the followers of Natural Law might approach the issues surrounding abortion b. "Natural Law has no serious weaknesses". Discuss	a. Explain the difference between the hypothetical and Categorical Imperative b. How useful is Kant's theory when considering embryo research?	See Just War question			a. Explain theories of ethical and religious pacifism b. Assess the claim that killing in war is more justifiable than other types of killing	See Kant question b.
Jan 2012	a. Explain the main differences between the Utilitarianism of Bentham and that of Mill b. "The Utilitarianism of Mill is superior in every way to that of Bentham". Discuss	a. Explain how Natural Law theory can be used to decide the right moral action b. To what extent is Natural Law the best approach to ethical decision-making?			a. Explain the main ethical principles of a religion you have studied with regard to genetic engineering b. "Religious ethics prevents progress in genetic engineering". Discuss	a. Explain how the concepts of personhood might influence ethical approaches to abortion b. "The right to life is the most important issue when considering abortion". Discuss		See religious ethics parts a. and b.
May 2012	a. X b. X	a. X b. X	a. X b. X	a. X b. X			a. X b. X	a. X b. X
Jan 2013	a. X b. X	a. X b. X			a. X b. X		a. X b. X	a. X b. X

73

Spot the gaps

It's likely that at least some students will have completed a January 2013 paper whilst reading this. If I was predicting which topic areas might come up in January 2013, I would pay close attention particularly to absolute/relative morality, as this area hasn't had explicit mention in any exam question for three papers. I would also suggest, simply on past trends, that genetic engineering was due for a mention. This isn't to suggest you neglect other areas, but simply to highlight that certain topic areas are more likely to come up if they haven't been examined on for some time.

The wording of the questions

Exam questions either examine a theory listed in the syllabus, or an applied issue, or they combine the two, with a specific theory (utilitarianism or natural law for example combined with pacifism).

Exam questions which ask you to explain a theory seem to follow a pattern.

1. Questions that ask you to explain some aspect of a theory. For example, you might be asked to explain Kant's Categorical Imperative, or Kant's idea of universalising moral precepts. You might be asked to explain Bentham's hedonic calculus, or Aquinas' idea of natural law as it relates to human purpose. Remember that the thing you're being asked to explain is always mentioned in the syllabus: you may be asked to explain the summum bonum in Kant, but not the idea of the noumenal realm in Kant.

2. Questions asking you to compare and contrast two theories or two aspects of the same general theory. For example, you might be asked to compare the Utilitarianism of Mill and Bentham, or explain the difference between a categorical and hypothetical imperative. You might be asked to explain the difference between a Natural Law and Kantian approach to explaining what is good, or between a teleological and deontological approach to deriving moral precepts. Finally, the difference between absolute and relative morality is an old favourite, so how about a question that asks you to explain the difference between absolute and relative approaches to moral decision-making?

3. Questions linking a theory to an application. These tend to follow the same wording. "Explain how a follower of Kant might approach issues surrounding abortion", or "explain how a natural law theorist might justify going to war".

4. Finally, be wary of a trick the examiner sometimes plays. I have stressed that the word "evaluate" only applies to part b. questions. In other words, in part a. questions you will only be asked to explain something for the 25 marks on offer out of 35. But how about the question "Explain the strengths of natural law theory"? Or "Explain the major weaknesses of utilitarian ethics"? You need to prepare to explain strengths and weaknesses as well as evaluate them (where evaluate here means say which you think are more or less valid strengths and weaknesses, and why).

• **REVISION TIP** - Make up your own exam questions using the type of wording mentioned above, for areas that the examiner has not yet asked about. You can use oft-repeated phrases like "issues surrounding".

Questions which only mention an application such as the right to a child in part a., though unusual, are possible (there were two in the May 2012 paper). Here the technique is to clearly define the issues surrounding that applied area. So as a student you should prepare very thoroughly the issues surrounding abortion, euthanasia, the right to a child, genetic engineering, and war and peace. Try to identify at least three.

- **REVISION TIP** - Prepare a grid with the issues on one axis and the major theories on the other. Fill in the squares with some key points, for example, on how a Kantian interprets the sanctity of human life with abortion or euthanasia, using the second formulation of the Categorical Imperative: "never use people just as a means to an end, but always, also as an end in themselves". You can then compare this with a natural law view of sanctity of human life and consider whether sanctity of life is possible when related to utilitarian ethics.

Part b questions

Part b questions tend to be harder as they include evaluation, and they are demanding because you only have 10-15 minutes to complete your answer (which is only worth 10/35 marks and so really needs to be concise to gain full marks). Many candidates spend too little time on part a (describing rather than explaining) and too much time on part b.

There is no time to waste on neat opening paragraphs as you must go straight to the heart of the issue. I would prepare by drawing up my own strengths and weaknesses tables and learning one or two quotes from key philosophers for each. I would also complete a sentence which started "the advantages of utilitarian ethics are .... because........" and trying to work out what my view is about the different theories. If you are evaluating you need to have a view which you can defend in a brief argument. The examiner continually stresses the need for evidence of **REFLECTION**.

- **REVISION TIP** - One minute debates are useful here. The teacher arranges chairs or desks in a circle with some students inside and some outside. The teacher then pre-prepares (or gets the class to pre-prepare) some "Discuss"questions. Then the students argue the case, the inner circle taking one view and the outer circle another (for and against the proposition). After one minute the whistle blows and the inner circle moves on one place.

  When the debate has been had four or five times, a plenary session can be held where we construct together the strongest case on either side. Then the students can vote on which side they prepare. Finally each student can be asked to write a paragraph justifying their view - which must have reasons to back the view up. A prize could awarded for the most analytical answer.

A2 PHILOSOPHY OF RELIGION (OCR G581)

At A2 there are no part a. and b. questions, so analysis and evaluation can intertwine seamlessly in your analysis. The key syllabus areas are:

- Religious Language

- Religious experience

- Miracle

- Attributes of God

- Life and Death

But notice that theories of revelation come in the Religious experience section of the syllabus, where a question may ask how God can reveal himself through sacred writings.

Note: The exact questions for June 2012 and January 2013 papers are still restricted by the exam board - for ten months after the exam. I have indicated the broad topic area by a cross. You should refer to the philosophicalinvestigations.co.uk website for exact wording - as soon as permitted, I will post them. Some crosses appear twice because questions may have an applied issue and a theory mentioned in the same question.

OCR G581	Religious Language	Religious experience	Miracle	Attributes of God	Life and Death
Jan 2010	Q4 Critically assess the views of Paul Tillich on religious language		Q2 A belief in miracles leads to the concept of a God who favours some but not of all of his creation. Discuss	Q1 Critically assess the philosophical problems raised by belief that God is omniscient	Q3 Evaluate the claim that there can be no disembodied existence after death
June 2010	Q1 Evaluate the claim that analogy can successfully be used to express the human understanding of God	Q3 Critically assess, with reference to William James, the argument from religious experience		Q2 Boethius was successful in his argument that God rewards and punishes justly. Discuss	Q4 To what extent is belief in an afterlife necessary for resolving problems raised by the existence of evil?
Jan 2011	Q1 To what extent can God reveal himself through sacred writings? Q2 Critically compare the use of myth with the use of analogy to express the human understanding of God		Q4 Evaluate Hume's claim that miracles are the least likely of events		Q3 Resurrection is more likely to be true than reincarnation.' Discuss
June 2011	Q1 Critically assess the claim that religious language is meaningless	Q4 Visions are not caused by God but can be explained by science.' Discuss		Q3 Critically assess the problems for believers who say that God is omniscient	Q2 Evaluate the claim that the soul is distinct from the body
Jan 2012	Q3 The falsification principle presents no real challenge to religious belief. Discuss	Q1 Corporate religious experiences prove the existence of God. Discuss	Q2 Critically assess the view that the concept of miracle is inconsistent with belief in a benevolent God	Q4 Assess the claim that the universe shows no evidence of the existence of a benevolent God	
June 2012	Q1 X	Q2 X		Q3 X	Q4 X
Jan 2013	Q1 X Via Negativa	Q2 X		Q3 X	Q4 X

Spot the gaps

Because the syllabus has only five sections it is important to analyse questions set within each syllabus area. However, it does seem that when one area is omitted (as it has to be each year with four questions set) then it is guaranteed to be examined upon next time. On this basis, it would seem more likely (though of course not certain) that in June 2013 the exam would include a question on miracles.

In order to get some idea of what question the examiner is likely to set on miracles, I would then analyse the twist given to each question in past years and then compare this with the twists suggested by the syllabus.

Jan 2010
- ✓ Miracles and God's partiality

June 2010
- ✓ No question

Jan 2011
- ✓ Hume's view evaluated

June 2011
- ✓ No question

Jan 2012
- ✓ Miracles and God's benevolence

What questions does this leave out, which have not been examined before on miracles? (That's not to suggest that we neglect past questions in our revision, of course). We arrive at the following list:

1. The biblical concept of miracle, linked to God's activity in the word. I would expect a question asking us to consider whether we can expect God's activity to be the same as that described in the Bible, or whether these ideas of miracles we find in the Bible are unique to the Biblical worldview, and why.

2. Criticisms of the concept of miracle raised by Maurice Wiles.

3. A question linking miracles to the problem of evil and the character of God - for example, "it is immoral for an omnipotent God to allow natural evil to persist".

4. A question asking whether modern people can possibly believe in miracles, such as "miracles are unbelievable in a scientific age" or "miracles only make sense within a pre-modern worldview".

5. A question with the phrase "critically compare", such as "critically compare the view of miracles taken by Hume and Wiles".

We will continue this analysis in the next chapter, where you should pay close attention to the twists, as I will call them, which I suggest the examiner may give to a question on a specific syllabus area.

Wording of questions

The wording of all A2 questions have a strong evaluative element within them. In fact the range of words used in exam questions are narrow.

"Critically assess" or "critically compare" occurred 10/24 times in our survey of questions from 2010 to 2012, meaning to weigh up arguments for this viewpoint and criticisms of the viewpoint, and crucially, then say which you think are valid or invalid and why (notice you are always supposed to come sort of firm conclusion to assess for an A grade. It is **NEVER** sufficient to say "there are strong arguments on both sides and so it ends up being a question of belief. Philosophy is always about developing a critical courage to come down in favour of one view or another, with reasons). As "critically compare" has only come as a command phrase once, it might be worth thinking which views could be compared within the syllabus. An obvious example is Hume's and Wiles' view of miracles.

- **REVISION TIP -** The more specific you make your revision the more useful it will be. For example, if you carefully revise the biblical view of miracles and set it alongside that of Hume and Wiles, and learn some quotes for each view, then this detailed knowledge can be used for any question on miracles. Whereas if you only revise general arguments, you will be caught out when the examiner asks a question naming a specific philosopher listed in the syllabus.

"Discuss" is used 7/24 times in our survey. Of course, to discuss means to evaluate and to analyse but a statement with discuss after it is more obviously biased one way or another. Illustrating this again from miracles, the statement "miracles are unbelievable" is obviously biased against the evidence for the miraculous, and will involve a discussion of both the concept of "miracle" and the idea of what it means to be "believable".

- **REVISION TIP -** Always practise unpacking key terms in an essay question, and do so critically. For example, the idea of miracle is ambiguous between "against natural law" and "improbable event" and it is only the former definition which offends against a scientific view. Science can handle improbability (such as the odd person has survived falling out of an aircraft at 10,000 feet, due to snowdrifts or a strong updraft) but science cannot accept impossibility (such as Jesus walking on water).

"Evaluate" is used 5/24 times. Evaluate means to consider what is good or bad about a particular view, what is valid or invalid in the argument or what is strong or weak about an argument. Evaluation can take place at different stages of the argument, and close attention should be paid to these different stages. For example, we can evaluate **definitions** as ambiguous or clear, we can evaluate **assumptions** as valid or invalid, and we can evaluate **arguments** as strong or weak and **conclusions** as logically following or logically not following an argument.

- **REVISION TIP -** Try to construct summary sheets that evaluate in this kind of way, by considering different definitions, the assumptions different philosophers make and the strength or otherwise of the argument that follows. Breaking it up this way forms a natural way of starting your essay. For example, in criticising Hume's view of miracles, we could say "Hume's definition is inadequate, his assumptions restrictive and the conclusion he therefore comes to is invalid".

"To what extent" is used twice as a command phrase to begin the question. This invites the answer "to some extent" or "completely" or "not at all". For example, if we are asked to what extent God reveals himself through sacred writings, we will need to argue either that this is only one of several ways God reveals himself, or to say that it is the only way and as such a complete, final revelation of God, or that God doesn't reveal himself at all through sacred writings. "To what extent" also invites a consideration of what exactly it is about God we can see in the Bible: God's character, actions, view of humanity and creation, the things God hates and loves: these are all relevant and require practice in taking a line on a question.

A2 ETHICS (OCR G582)

There are five broad areas in the A2 syllabus for Ethics. But we should note that ethical theories studied at AS level, of Natural Law, Kant, Utilitarianism (in its three forms), and Religious Ethics can still feature in exam questions (and have been specifically named three times). The examiner also mentions "ethical theories" as a general term, which invites you to choose which you think are strong and which weak on any issue. It's worth preparing your (carefully reasoned) view on this: do you prefer Virtue Ethics or Kant, for example?

Note: The exact questions for June 2012 and January 2013 papers are still restricted by the exam board - for ten months after the exam. I have indicated the broad topic area by a cross. You should refer to the philosophicalinvestigations.co.uk website for exact wording - as soon as permitted, I will post them. Some crosses appear twice because questions may have an applied issue and a theory mentioned in the same question.

OCR G582	Meta-ethics	Free will	Conscience	Virtue	Env and Bus	Sexual Ethics
Jan 2010	To what extent is ethical language meaningful?		Assess the view that conscience need not always be obeyed		'Utilitarianism is not the best approach to environmental issues'. Discuss	'Some ethical theories are more useful than others when making decisions about sexual ethics'. Discuss
June 2010		Critically assess the claim that people are free to make moral decisions		"The weaknesses of Virtue Ethics outweigh its strengths". Discuss	Assess the usefulness of Religious Ethics as an ethical approach to business.	To what extent are ethical theories helpful when considering the issues surrounding homosexuality?
Jan 2011		Our ethical decisions are merely the result of social conditioning'. Discuss	Critically assess the claim that conscience is the voice of reason		"The environment suffers because business has no ethics". Discuss	Natural law is the most reliable approach when making decisions about premarital sex". Discuss
June 2011	"Ethical statements are no more than expressions of emotion". Discuss	Critically assess the view that we are not responsible for our evil actions		To what extent is Virtue Ethics helpful when making decisions about extramarital sex?	Assess the claim that secular approaches to environmental issues are of more help than religious approaches	
Jan 2012	"All ethical language is prescriptive". Discuss	See sexual ethics question	Critically assess the claim that free will and determinism are compatible	To what extent do modern versions of Virtue Ethics address the weaknesses of Aristotle's teaching?		"For moral issues surrounding sex the demands of conscience override other ethical considerations". Discuss
June 2012	X	X	X	X	X Business ethics X Environmental ethics	
Jan 2013			X	X	X Business	X

Spot the gaps

Where one area is missed out in one paper it is usually examined in some form in the next paper set. On this basis, I expected Virtue Ethics, Sexual Ethics and Free Will to have featured in questions in January 2013. But a thorough analysis of the specification also tells us that some themes in the syllabus have never been examined. This makes them more likely the longer they stay absent. For example, the issue of contraception has never featured in an exam question. There are also particular slants on a familiar topic area which have never been examined. Go to the next chapter to find out what they are.

Students often ask me if they can safely leave a topic area out altogether (the least favourite one being Meta-ethics). The answer is probably "yes" to this, as long as the strategies for handling any topic area suggested in this book are followed. Leave out Meta-ethics (for example) and you will still have three questions to choose from as long as the examiner doesn't repeat what happened in June 2012 - where two questions were set on the one syllabus area "environmental and business ethics".

Having said that: if you can master Meta-ethics the questions are really quite predictable, and usually revolve around a core issue - which theory best makes sense of ethical statements. You can attack emotivism fairly hard as few people these days see much validity in AJ Ayer's view, whereas a theory like Prescriptivism would seem to be truer to how we use moral language. Remember too that naturalism (objective basis for ethical statements) has made a comeback and so an answer defending naturalism against the naturalistic fallacy attack makes for an interesting essay which will stand out in this less popular topic area.

Wording of the questions

"Critically assess" and "assess" are favourite command words, also "to what extent", and a deliberately slanted comment followed by "Discuss". Essentially the technique is the same: to analyse theories and applications in a logical way and to point out strengths and weaknesses in a position as you go along. Unlike AS level, where part a. questions ask you to explain something and part b. to evaluate, here the evaluation and analysis should be woven together. Some ideas of how you can practise this for an exam are given in the final chapter of the book.

Ambiguities

My own view is that the Environmental and Business Ethics section is the least well thought out, and this perhaps explains why it hasn't been a popular area for examiners in the past. Part of the difficulty is that we have two areas of ethics which traditionally are dealt with separately and here they are placed together. There are linkages, of course. "The environment suffers because business has no ethics" might well be the view of many people. I prefer to teach this area looking at case studies of poor business practice and then applying a Kantian/ Natural Law/ Utilitarian / Virtue Ethics approach to issues that emerge. A core issue here is whether any ethical theory really addresses environmental issues, or whether we have to take refuge in the metaphysics of Gaia to make sense of the innate value of the environment.

Revision tip: Use real examples from the newspaper which are provided by the philosophicalinvestigations website or from your own research. There are some good films based on real life events, such as Erin Brokovitch and the Constant Gardener. Recent cases include Glencore and Trafigura. Try to establish the motive of managers in these cases, and whether a study of ethical theories would have helped them.

How to Bring Specification and Past Questions Together

The specification gives an outline of the topics examined, and the subdivisions within the specification tell us which "twists" (as I call them) to expect. By lining up past questions against the specification we also get a clearer idea how to interpret the specification, and hence this allows us to predict more accurately questions in the future.

In this chapter we will break the specification down into subunits and then match questions to each subdivision. Possible future questions are indicated by a star, past questions already set, by a tick.

Please note: we cannot reproduce May 2012 and Jan 2013 questions exactly, until ten months after the exam. I have given a general indication of the area examined in May and January, and also in the table indicated those areas examined in these two papers with a cross.

AS PHILOSOPHY OF RELIGION (OCR G571)

Plato: The analogy of the cave

▸ **The Republic VII. 514A–521B**

Candidates should be able to demonstrate knowledge and understanding of what might be represented in the Analogy of the Cave by the following:

▸ **The prisoners, the shadows, the cave itself, the outside world, the sun, the journey out of the cave and the return to the prisoners**

June 2009 (a & b)

✓ Explain the analogy of the cave in Plato's Republic

✓ 'The analogy of the cave tells us nothing about reality'. Discuss

Possible future question (Jan 2013 part a & b was similar to this)

★ Explain the meaning of the different elements in Plato's analogy of the cave.

★ To what extent is the analogy of the cave a useful explanation of reality?

Plato: The concept of the forms; the form of the good

Candidates should understand what Plato meant by 'Forms' and be able to demonstrate knowledge and understanding of:

▸ **The relation between concepts and phenomena**

Possible future question (a & b)

★ Explain the relationship between concepts and phenomena in Plato's thought

★ 'Plato's thought has useful things to teach us about reality". Discuss

▸ **The concept of "Ideals"**

Jan 2010 (a & b)

✓ Explain the concept of Ideals in Plato's writings

✓ 'Ideals are an illusion; we can only experience what is real'. Discuss

▸ **The relation between the Form of the Good and the other Forms**

Possible future question (a & b)

★ Explain the relationship between the Form of the good and other forms in Plato's teaching

★ "The Form of the good is too abstract to bear any relation to reality". Discuss

Aristotle: Ideas about cause in purpose in relation to God (Metaphysics book 12)

▸ **Aristotle's understanding of material, efficient, formal and final cause**

June 2009 (a & b)

✓ Explain what Aristotle meant by final cause

✓ To what extent does the concept of final cause teach us anything about the real world

June 2011 (a & b)

✓ Asked a question about the four causes in Aristotle

✓ Required us to evaluate the four causes as a description of reality

The examiner commented of student answers to part b. "Far too many candidates took little notice of the assumptions surrounding the notion of the Final Cause", and of part a. noted that "too many students confuse Aristotle and Aquinas".

▸ **Aristotle's concept of the Prime Mover**

Possible future question (a & b)

★ Explain Aristotle's concept of the Prime Mover

★ To what extent is the Prime Mover an adequate explanation of divine activity?

Note: the examiner makes this comment about Aristotle's empiricism on Q4b June 2012 "Many candidates argued that there was no physical evidence for the Forms, many attempted to describe the Third Man argument of Aristotle though relatively few made use of any of his detailed, and rather simpler, criticisms in Nicomachean Ethics Book I, Chapter vi."

Judaeo-Christian influences on philosophy of religion

Candidates should be familiar with Biblical texts to exemplify the topics below. There are no prescribed texts.

▸ **The concept of God as creator**

▸ **The way the Bible presents God as involved with his creation;**

Possible future question (a & b)

★ Explain what the Bible means by a Creator God involved with his creation

★ "The Biblical account of God as Creator cannot be reconciled with scientific views of reality". Discuss

▸ **The imagery of God as a craftsman**

June 2010 (a & b)

✓ Compare the concept of God as Prime Mover with the idea of God as craftsman

✓ "Only philosophers can explain creation". Discuss

- ▸ **The concepts of omnipotence, omniscience and omnipresence**

  Possible future question (a & b)

  ★ Explain how God's omnipotence can coexist with God's benevolence

  ★ If God knows everything how can evil exist?

- ▸ **The concept of "creatio ex nihilo"**

  Jan 2010 (a & b)

  ✓ Explain the concept of "Creatio ex nihilo"

  ✓ "Nothing comes from nothing". Discuss

- ▸ **Compare this view with Aristotle's Prime Mover**

  Possible future question (a & b)

  ★ Compare and contrast Aristotle's idea of Prime Mover with the idea of God as Creator in the Judaeo-Christian tradition

  ★ "God is involved with his Creation". Discuss

  Possible part b. question

  ★ "God who made the world is responsible for everything that happens". Discuss

The goodness of God

▸ **The ways in which the God of the Bible is seen as morally perfect and the source of human ethics**

Jan 2011 (a & b)

✓ Explain what it means to say that 'God is good'

✓ To what extent are things only good because God commands them?

▸ **The concept of God as lawgiver and as judge**

Jan 2009 (a & b)

✓ Explain the Judaeo-Christian concept of God as law-giver and judge

✓ 'God has no right to judge human beings'. Discuss

▸ **Consider whether, in a Biblical context, God commands things because they are good or whether things are good because God commands them**

Jan 2012 (a & b)

✓ Explain biblical beliefs about the attributes of God

✓ "The Bible is too inconsistent to be used for moral teachings". Discuss

Traditional arguments for the existence of God

▸ **The Ontological argument from Anselm and Descartes**

June 2010 (a & b)

✓ Explain Anselm's ontological argument

✓ "It is pointless to deny the logical necessity of the existence of God". Discuss

▸ **Challenges to it from Gaunilo and Kant**

May 2012 (a & b)

★ Copyright OCR board embargoed until April 2012.

Possible future questions (a & b)

★ Explain how Kant challenged the ontological argument

★ To what extent was Kant successful in his criticisms of the ontological argument?Anselm's understanding of God – his understanding of the differences between contingent and necessary existence

Possible future question (a & b)

★ Explain Anselm's distinction between necessary and contingent existence

★ "Only God necessarily exists; everything else is contingent". Discuss

▸ **Descartes' understanding of existence as a perfection which God cannot lack**

Possible future question (a & b)

★ Explain Descartes' version of the ontological argument

★ "Descartes' argument is ultimately unconvincing". Discuss

▸ **Gaunilo's analogy of the island in On Behalf of the Fool**

Possible future question (a & b)

★ Explain how Gaunilo's analogy of the island affects Anselm's ontological argument

★ "Gaunilo's analogy of the island is fatal to Anselm's argument". Discuss

The cosmological argument from Aquinas and Copleston; challenges from Hume and Russell

▸ **The Cosmological argument from Aquinas and Copleston**

June 2009 (a & b)

✓ Explain Aquinas' cosmological argument

✓ To what extent were Russell's criticisms of the Cosmological argument successful

▸ **The arguments put forward by Copleston in the 1948 radio debate with Russell and Russell's counter arguments**

Jan 2012 (a & b)

✓ Explain the arguments put forward by Copleston in his radio debate with Russell

✓ How far was Russell successful in countering Copleston's argument in the radio debate?

▸ **Hume's criticisms of the cosmological argument**

May 2011 (a & b)

✓ Explain Hume's criticisms of the cosmological argument

✓ To what extent was Hume successful in his critique of the cosmological argument?

The examiner commented on part a: "Some candidates were able to explain Hume's observation of the role of habit in linking cause to effect, which a few excellent answers were able to identify as the fallacy of affirmation of the consequent. Bertrand Russell was used regularly and to good effect as a development of Hume's ideas on infinite regress".

The Teleological argument from Aquinas and Paley; challenges from Hume, Mill and Darwin

▸ **The teleological argument from Aquinas and Paley**

June 2011 (a & b)
- ✓ Explain Paley's argument for the existence of God
- ✓ 'The universe has no purpose'. Discuss

Possible future question (a & b)
- ★ Explain Aquinas' argument for the existence of God
- ★ "Aquinas' argument is unconvincing". Discuss

▸ **The challenges to it from Hume, Mill and Darwinism**

Jan 2010 (a & b)
- ✓ Explain Mill's challenges to the teleological argument
- ✓ Evaluate the claim that the universe has too many flaws to be designed

Jan 2013 (a & b) asked us to consider Mill's challenges and evaluate.

Possible future question (a & b)
- ★ Explain how Darwinism challenges the teleological argument
- ★ "Darwin's challenges to the teleological argument are unconvincing'. Discuss

The moral argument from Kant: Psychological challenges from Freud

▸ **The moral argument from Kant, including his concept of the 'summum bonum' and his inferences about innate moral awareness**

June 2009 (a & b)

✓ Explain Kant's moral argument for the existence of God

✓ "Moral awareness has nothing to do with God". Discuss

Possible future question (a & b)

★ Explain Kant's view that moral awareness is innate

★ "Moral awareness is a product of our upbringing'. Discuss

Jan 2011 (a & b)

✓ Explain what Kant means by 'summum bonum'

✓ "The existence of morality is not evidence for the existence of God". Discuss

▸ **Psychological challenges from Freud to the moral argument, his view that moral awareness comes from sources other than God**

June 2010 (a & b) and Jan 2013 (a & b) was very similar

✓ Explain Freud's view that moral awareness comes from sources other than God

✓ "God is the only explanation of moral awareness". Discuss

Challenges to religious belief: The problem of evil

▸ The problem of evil: the classic theodicies of Augustine and Irenaeus

June 2009 (a & b)

✓ Explain why Irenaeus argues that the existence of evil is a necessary part of the universe

✓ "Irenaeus is wrong : evil disproves the existence of God". Discuss

May 2011 (a & b)

✓ Explain the Irenaen theodicy

✓ To what extent can evil be said to be simply a test?

The examiner commented on part a. answers: A number of candidates were able to make good use of the 'image'/'likeness' distinction found in Genesis 1:26. Better responses explored the way that virtues could be developed towards the likeness of God (in a much more Hickean way). It was pleasing to see some candidates identifying the link between the immaturity of Adam and Eve with Irenaeus' explanation of why man was not made perfect from the beginning through the analogy of a mother giving a child milk.

Possible future question (a & b)

★ Explain Augustinian theodicy

★ "Augustine fails to provide a convincing explanation for the existence of evil". Discuss

▸ The nature of the problem of evil and the possible differences between natural and moral evil

Jan 2011 (a & b)

- ✓ Explain the nature of the problem of evil
- ✓ "Moral evil may be the fault of humanity but natural evil is God's fault". Discuss

▸ **How each theodicy understands the responsibility of God for the existence of evil in the world**

Possible future question (a & b)

- ★ Explain how the theodicies of Augustine and Irenaeus understand God's responsibility for evil
- ★ "The existence of evil cannot be explained adequately by theodicy". Discuss

▸ **The origins of evil and the role of human free will**

Possible future question (a & b)

- ★ Explain the origins of evil
- ★ "Evil is purely a result of human free will". Discuss

Religion and science

▸ **Scientific and philosophical views on the creation of the universe; particularly the debate between Creationism and the Big Bang theory**

June 2009 (a & b)

✓ Explain the debate between Creationism and Big Bang Theory

✓ 'The big bang theory is more believable than creationism'. Discuss

Jan 2011 (a & b)

✓ Explain why some creationists do not believe in big bang theory

✓ 'Scientists are the only ones who can explain why the universe is here'. Discuss

▸ **Darwinism and various developments of evolutionary theory**

Jan 2010 (a & b) and Jan 2013 (a & b) was very similar

✓ Explain Darwinism and evolutionary theory

✓ 'The universe is too complex for evolutionary theory to explain it'. Discuss

▸ **"Intelligent Design" and "Irreducible Complexity"**

June 2010 (a & b)

✓ Explain the concept of irreducible complexity

✓ 'There is no evidence of intelligent design in the universe'. Discuss

Possible future question (a & b)

★ Explain the idea of intelligent design

★ "Intelligent design is unconvincing as a theory". Discuss

▸ **Religious responses to challenges posed by scientific views**

Jan 2012 (a & b)

✓ Compare scientific and philosophical views on the creation of the universe

✓ Evaluate the view that science can only explain how and not why the universe exists

AS ETHICS (OCR G572)

In this section we relate past questions (with the date set) to the specification and then consider which areas have not been examined on before. Possible future questions are marked below.

General terms

▸ Absolute and relative

Jan 2010 (a & b)

✓ Explain what is meant by moral absolutism

✓ 'Moral absolutism cannot be justified'. Discuss

June 2010 (a & b)

✓ Explain the differences between absolute and relative morality

✓ 'Relativism can give no convincing reasons why people should be good' Discuss

Jan 2011 Asks us to link relativism to abortion issues and discuss whether the outcome is immoral.

▸ Absolute and objective

This link has not been examined to June 2012 although Jan 2013 did ask us to explain generally the idea of absolute morality.

Possible future question (a & b)

★ Explain to what extent absolute ethical theories are also objective

★ "Objective ethical theories mean that the truth applies everywhere, for all time". Discuss

▸ Relative and subjective

This link has not been examined up to Jan 2013.

Possible future question (a & b)

★ Explain to what extent relative ethical theories are necessarily subjective

★ "A relativist inevitably sees issues surrounding euthanasia as a subjective choice". Discuss

▸ Deontological and teleological

May 2012 (part a) and Jan 2013 (part b)

✓ Asks us in part a. to contrast deontological and teleological ethics

✓ Jan 2013 asks us to compare rules and consequences

Possible future questions (a & b)

★ Explain the difference between subjective and objective theories of ethics

★ "Only objective theories of ethics are useful when considering issues surrounding abortion". Discuss

★ Explain how an ethical theory you have studied may be considered subjective

★ "Subjective theories of ethics are of no use in solving ethical dilemmas". Discuss

Ethical theories: Natural law

▸ **Link Aquinas' theory to Aristotle's idea of Natural Purpose**

Possible future question (a & b)

★ Explain how Aquinas' Natural law theory uses Aristotle's idea of Natural Human Purpose

★ "Natural Law theory has an unrealistic view of human nature" Discuss

▸ **Consider Aquinas' view of purpose and eudaimonia (excellence or perfection)**

Possible future question (a & b)

★ Explain how Aquinas' Natural Law theory links natural purpose to eudaimonia

★ "Eudaimonia is inevitably subjective". Discuss

▸ **Examine how Natural law theory is linked to human reason**

Jan 2012 (a & b)

✓ Explain how Natural Law theory can be used to decide the right moral action

✓ To what extent is Natural Law the best approach to ethical decision-making?.

Possible future question (a & b)

★ Explain how Natural law theory could be described as reasonable

★ "Natural Law theory leads to unreasonable outcomes". Discuss

▸ **Thoroughly understand and explain primary and secondary precepts**

Possible future question (a & b)

★ Explain the difference between primary and secondary precepts in Natural Law

★ "Primary precepts are absolute, but secondary precepts are relative". Discuss

▸ **Consider each of these critically and assess their strengths and weaknesses**

Jan 2010 (a & b) and Jan 2013 (a & b) also linked Natural Law to embryo research

✓ Explain the strengths of Natural Law theory

✓ To what extent would a follower of Natural Law accept embryo research

May 2011 (a & b)

✓ Explain how the followers of Natural Law might approach the issues surrounding abortion

✓ "Natural Law has no serious weaknesses". Discuss

Possible future question (a & b)

★ Explain how Natural Law theory might address issues surrounding genetic engineering

★ "Natural Law's strengths outweigh its weaknesses". Discuss

Ethical theories: Kantian ethics

▸ **Consider the differences between the hypothetical and categorical imperatives**

Jan 2011 (part a)

✓ Explain Kant's argument for using the Categorical Imperative (notice, this is a slightly different question from "explain Kant's Categorical Imperative")

✓ "The universalisation of maxims by Kant cannot be defended". Discuss

May 2011 (a & b)

✓ Explain the difference between the hypothetical and categorical imperative

✓ How useful is the categorical imperative when applied to embryo research?

Possible future question (a & b)

★ Explain how Kant's Categorical Imperative must be absolute

★ "Absolute imperatives lead to immoral outcomes". Discuss

▸ **Know about different ways of expressing the one Categorical Imperative**

Possible future question (a & b)

★ Explain two variations of Kant's Categorical Imperative

★ "The Categorical Imperative is difficult to apply to issues surrounding abortion". Discuss

▸ Know how to explain "universalisation of maxims"

Notice that there are two key terms here, universalisation (or universalisability as it's more usually called) and the idea of a maxim. It's worth considering what is meant by a **MAXIM**.

Jan 2011 (a & b)

✓ Explain Kant's argument for using the Categorical Imperative (notice, this is a slightly different question from "explain Kant's Categorical Imperative")

✓ "The universalisation of maxims by Kant cannot be defended". Discuss

Possible future question (a & b)

★ Explain how Kant establishes the universalisation of ethical maxims

★ "Universalisable maxims must be absolute". Discuss

▸ Consider what duty might mean in the context of Kant's ethics

The word "duty" has never come up in an exam question, so we should expect it sometime.

Possible future question (a & b)

★ Explain what Kant meant by always doing our "duty for duty's sake"

★ "The idea of duty is over-restrictive". Discuss

▸ Consider Kant's ideas of "moral law", "good will" and "summum bonum"

These are three technical terms which have not been used before in exam questions - so we might expect them.

Possible future questions (a & b)

★ Explain Kant's idea of the summum bonum

★ "The motive of duty is incompatible with the end of the summum bonum". Discuss

★ Explain what Kant meant by "the good will"

★ "Kant places motive above consequences". Discuss

★ Explain how Kant establishes the idea of the moral law

★ "Legalistic theories are of no use when considering issues surrounding abortion". Discuss

Ethical theories: Utilitarianism

▸ **Consider Bentham and Mill's versions of Utilitarianism**

Jan 2012 (a & b)

✓ Explain the differences between the Utilitarianism of Bentham and Mill

✓ 'The Utilitarianism of Mill is superior in every way to that of Bentham'. Discuss

Possible future question (a & b)

★ Explain how Mill develops Bentham's idea of Utilitarianism (note: Jan 2013 asked us specifically about Mill's Utilitarianism)

★ "Mill's version of Utilitarianism is superior to Bentham's". Discuss

▸ **Compare and contrast the two theories**

Jan 2012 (a & b)

✓ (as above) Asks us in part a. to explain the differences between Mill's and Bentham's versions and then in part b. to discuss whether Mill's is superior (as mentioned above)

▸ **Consider the hedonic calculus of Bentham, and Mill's qualitative pleasures, and the difference between Act and Rule Utilitarianism**

Jan 2011 (a & b)

✓ Explain the difference between Act and Rule Utilitarianism

✓ To what extent is Utilitarianism useful in making decisions about euthanasia?

★ Explain the difference between higher and lower pleasures in the Utilitarianism of Bentham and Mill

★ "The idea of pleasure is of no practical use when considering issues surrounding euthanasia". Discuss

★ Explain how Bentham's hedonic calculus might be applied by a person considering an abortion

★ "Teleological theories are superior to deontological theories when making practical decisions". Discuss

▶ **Consider the Preference Utilitarianism of Peter Singer**

May 2011 (a & b)

✓ Explain the Preference Utilitarianism of Peter Singer

✓ To what extent is Preference Utilitarianism the best form of Utilitarianism?

Possible future question (a & b)

★ Explain how a Preference Utilitarian might approach issues surrounding abortion

★ "Preference Utilitarianism leads to immoral outcomes". Discuss

▶ **Critical assessment and strengths and weaknesses**

May 2012 (a & b)

✓ Part a was linked to Mill's version.

✓ Part b. asked us to evaluate Utilitarianism.

Jan 2010 (part a)

✓ Explain how Utilitarians approach the issues of war

Ethical theories: Religious ethics

▸ **Consider the principles of our chosen religion and how followers make decisions**

Jan 2011 (a & b)

✓ Explain how a follower of any religion makes ethical decisions

✓ "Religion and morality are separate". Discuss

▸ **Understand how morality and religion are or are not linked**

Jan 2011 (a & b as above)

✓ Explain how a follower of any religion makes ethical decisions

✓ "Morality and religion are separate". Discuss

▸ **Consider how far morality depends on God, as in Divine Command Theory**

Possible future questions (a & b)

★ Explain how far morality depends on God of a religion you have studied

★ "Morality must depend on reason, not God". Discuss

★ Explain how the followers of religion you have studied take ethical decisions

★ "Religious ethics must originate in God's commands", Discuss

- **Links the idea of religious ethics to the concepts of absolute and relative ethics**

Possible future question (a & b)

★ Explain whether the ethics of a religion you have studied should be described as absolute or relative

★ "Religious Ethics can lead to immoral outcomes". Discuss

- **Consider how ethical theories (we assume the specification means theories such as such as Natural Law, Kantian ethics) can be considered "religious"**

For example, I interpret this as asking is Kant's theory a religious ethical theory or not? Is Natural Law by definition "religious"?

Possible future question (a & b)

★ Explain how we might describe a particular moral theory as "religious"

★ "All morality derives from God". Discuss

- **Critical assessment and strengths and weaknesses**

June 2010 (a & b)

✓ Explain the ethical religious principles involved in war

✓ "War should not be allowed under any circumstances". Discuss

May 2012 (a & b)

✓ Part a. asks us to consider how religious ethics handles decisions about going to war

✓ Part b. asks us to discuss whether all religious people should inevitably be pacifist

Jan 2010 (a & b)

✓ Explain how the ethics of a religion you have studied might be applied to abortion

✓ "Religious ethics fail to consider the consequences". Discuss

Jan 2012 (a & b)

✓ Explain the main ethical principles of a religion you have studied with regard to genetic engineering

✓ "Religious ethics prevents progress in genetic engineering". Discuss

Possible future questions (a & b)

★ Explain the main ethical principles of a religion you have studied with regard to euthanasia

★ "Religious ethics causes unnecessary suffering". Discuss

★ Explain the main ethical principles of a religion you have studied with regard to the issues surrounding a right to a child

★ "Children are the gift of God". Discuss

★ Explain the major strengths of a religious ethic you have studied

★ "The strengths of religious ethics outweigh their weaknesses". Discuss

Applied ethics: Abortion - the right to a child

▸ **Consider the sanctity of life**

Possible future question (a & b)

★ Explain how the concept of the sanctity of life affects issues surrounding abortion

★ "The foetus is a human person". Discuss

▸ **Understand the concept of personhood**

Jan 2012 (part a)

✓ Explain how concepts of personhood influence ethical approaches to abortion

▸ **Apply the idea of "right to life" to abortion**

Jan 2012 (part b)

✓ "The right to life is the most important factor when considering issues surrounding abortion". Discuss

Possible part b question

★ "The foetus has a right to life". Discuss

▸ **Examine issues around infertility and the idea of a "right to a child"**

Note, don't muddle up abortion and right to a child although they are in the same syllabus area. In June 2012 the examiner notes "some candidates struggled with the concept 'right to a child' and attempted responses which focused on the issue of abortion"

June 2010 (a & b)

- ✓ Explain how a follower of Kantian ethics might approach the issues surrounding the right to a child
- ✓ "The right to a child is an absolute right". Discuss

May 2012 (part a)

- ✓ Asks us in a part a. question to explain, in general terms, the issues surrounding a right to a child

Possible part b. question

- ★ "The right to a child is a meaningless concept". Discuss

‣ **Determine whether a child is a gift or a right**

June 2010 (part b)

- ✓ "The right to a child is an absolute right". Discuss

May 2012 (part b)

- ✓ Asks us to discuss in a part b. question whether a child is a gift not a right

‣ **Apply the ethical theories of Kant, Utilitarianism, Natural law and Religious Ethics to abortion and right to a child**

The syllabus suggests issues of personhood, rights and sanctity of life are three that should be considered).

Jan 2010 (part a)

- ✓ Explain how the ethics of a religion you have studied might be applied to abortion

Jan 2011 (part a)

✓ Explain how a moral relativist might approach issues raised by abortion

May 2011 (part a)

✓ Explain how a follower of Natural Law might approach the issues surrounding abortion

Possible future question (a & b)

★ Explain how the follower of a religion (substitute a Kantian or Utilitarian here) might approach issues surrounding the right to a child

★ "Children are the gift of God". Discuss

Applied ethics: Euthanasia

▸ **Apply sanctity of life to euthanasia**

Possible future question (a & b)

★ Explain how a Natural Law theorist might argue for the sanctity of human life

★ "Sanctity of life is more important than quality of life". Discuss

▸ **Apply quality of life to euthanasia**

May 2012 (part b)

✓ Part b. asks us to consider whether quality of life is the key thing to consider when thinking about euthanasia

▸ **Apply right to life to euthanasia**

Possible future question (part b)

★ "The right to life includes the right to choose your own death". Discuss

▸ **Link the approaches of the ethical theories of Kant, Natural law, Utilitarianism and religious Ethics to euthanasia**

Jan 2011 (part b)

✓ To what extent is Utilitarianism a useful method of making decisions about euthanasia?

May 2012 (part a)

✓ Asks us in part a. to explain the ethical issues surrounding euthanasia and then asks us in part b. to discuss whether the end ever justifies the means.

Applied ethics: Genetic engineering

▸ **Apply genetic engineering to humans, animals and embryos and understand the issues**

Jan 2010 (part b) and Jan 2013 (part a made this same link to embryos)

✓ To what extent could the followers of Natural law accept embryo research

▸ **Link Kant, Natural law, Utilitarianism and Religious Ethics to issues raised by genetic engineering**

Jan 2010 (part b)

✓ Asks us in part b. to discuss whether the followers of Natural law could accept embryo research (see above)

Applied ethics: War and peace

▸ **Understand and apply Just War principles**

Possible future (a & b) - Jan 2013 in fact asked a straightforward question on Just War Principles

★ Explain how a follower of a religion you have studied creates principles of Just War

★ "War is never justified". Discuss

▸ **Understand theories of ethical and religious pacifism**

May 2011 (a & b)

✓ Explain the theories of ethical and religious pacifism

✓ Assess the claim that killing in war is more justifiable than other types of killing.

May 2012 (a & b)

✓ Asks us in part a. to explain how followers of a religion justify war and then in part b. asks us to discuss whether religious followers should be pacifist.

▸ **Discuss how Kant, Natural law Theory, Utilitarianism and Religious Ethics might handle issues of war and peace**

Jan 2010 (a & b)

✓ Explain how Utilitarians approach issues of war

✓ "Pacifism does more harm than good". Discuss

June 2010 (a & b)

✓ Explain the ethical principles of a religion you have studied in relation to war.

✓ "War should not be allowed even as a last resort". Discuss

Possible future question (a & b)

★ Explain how a Kantian might justify going to war

★ "There can be no hard and fast rules about going to war". Discuss

A2 PHILOSOPHY OF RELIGION (OCR G581)

In this section we relate past questions (with the date set) to the specification and then consider which areas have not been examined on before. Possible future questions are marked below.

Religious language

▸ **Religious language – uses and purpose**

▸ **The via negativa (Apophatic way)**

Possible future question

★ Critically assess how the via negativa establishes the meaningfulness of religious language

▸ **The verification and falsification principles**

Jan 2012

✓ The falsification principle presents no real challenge to religious belief. Discuss

Possible future question

★ "The verification principle presents a serious threat to religious belief". Discuss

▸ **Different views on the meaningfulness of religious language**

June 2011

✓ Critically assess the claim that religious language is meaningless

▸ **The uses of symbol, analogy and myth to express human understanding of God**

June 2010

✓ Evaluate the claim that analogy can successfully be used to express the human understanding of God

Jan 2011

✓ Critically compare the use of myth with the use of analogy to express the human understanding of God

Possible future questions

★ Critically compare the use of analogy with the use of symbol to express the human understanding of God

★ Evaluate the claim that symbol can be successfully used to express the human understanding of God

▸ **The views of the Vienna Circle, A. J. Ayer, Anthony Flew, Ludwig Wittgenstein and Paul Tillich on religious language**

Jan 2010

✓ Critically assess the views of Paul Tillich on Religious Language

May 2012

✓ Asked us to do an evaluation of Wittgenstein's theory

Possible future questions

★ Critically assess Ayer's view that religious language is meaningless

★ Compare and evaluate Ayer's and Flew's views of the meaningfulness of religious language

★ Assess the strengths of Anthony Flew's views of religious language

Religious experience

Candidates should be able to demonstrate knowledge and understanding of the following in relation to God and religious belief:

▸ **Arguments from religious experience from William James**

June 2010

✓ Critically assess, with reference to William James, the argument from religious experience

▸ **The aims and main conclusions drawn by William James in The Varieties of Religious Experience**

Possible future question

★ Critically assess William James' conclusions regarding the validity of religious experiences

▸ **The following different forms of religious experience: visions, voices, 'numinous' experience, conversion experience, corporate religious experience**

June 2011

✓ "Visions are not caused by God but can be explained by science". Discuss

Jan 2012

✓ "Corporate religious experiences prove the existence of God". Discuss

May 2012

✓ Asked a question on conversion experiences and belief in God.

Possible future questions

★ Critically assess the role of numinous experiences in producing faith in God

★ "Visions are essentially subjective, so prove nothing regarding God's existence". Discuss

▶ **The concept of revelation through sacred writings**

Jan 2011

✓ To what extent can God reveal himself through sacred writings?

Note: the examiner comments on the question above (Jan 2011 Q1:) "a disappointingly large number of candidates failed to understand the nature of propositional and non-propositional approaches, arguing that the first implied direct revelation (normally literal) and the latter indirect revelation. Neither definition is correct. Very many failed to recognise that in the life of believers, both aspects are frequently present".

Possible future questions

★ Critically assess different models of revelation through sacred writings within a religious tradition

★ "Sacred writings are inevitably culture-bound". Discuss

Miracle

A study of how God might interact with humanity, by looking at the concept of miracle.

▸ **Different definitions of miracle, including an understanding of Hume**

▸ **The biblical concept of miracle and the issues this raises about God's activity in the world**

Possible future questions

★ Critically assess the biblical concept of miracle and the issues it raises about God's activity in the world

▸ **The concept of miracle, and criticisms made by Hume and Wiles**

Jan 2011

✓ Evaluate Hume's claim that miracles are the least likely of events

The examiner wrote of the answers to this question: "A surprising number thought – contrary to Hume's own account - that he claimed the laws of nature were fixed and unbreakable, with miracles impossible".

Possible future question

★ Evaluate Wiles' claim that the absence of widespread miracles makes it improbable that God exists

- **The implications of the concept of miracle for the problem of evil**

Jan 2012

✓ Critically assess the view that the concept of miracle is inconsistent with a belief in a benevolent God

Possible future questions

★ "An all powerful God would miraculously prevent all forms of natural evil". Discuss

★ "The lack of evidence for miracles proves that God cannot be benevolent". Discuss

- **Candidates should be able to discuss whether modern people can be expected to believe in miracles, and whether miracles suggest an arbitrary or partisan God**

Jan 2010

✓ "A belief in miracles leads to the concept of a God who favours some but not all of his creation". Discuss

Possible future questions

★ "A belief in the miraculous cannot be reconciled with a scientific worldview". Discuss

★ "A belief in miracles suggests a primitive worldview". Discuss

Nature of God

▶ **God as eternal, omniscient, omnipotent and omni-benevolent – and the philosophical problems arising from these concepts**

Jan 2010

✓ Critically assess the philosophical problems raised by belief that God is omniscient

May 2011

✓ Critically assess the problems for believers who say that God is omniscient

Jan 2012

✓ Assess the claim that the universe shows no evidence of the existence of God

June 2012

✓ Evaluate the philosophical problems raised by the belief that God is eternal

Possible future question

★ "God's omnipotence is not compatible with his omnibenevolence". Discuss

▶

▸ **The views of Boethius in his discussion of eternity and God's foreknowledge in Book 5 of The Consolations of Philosophy**

June 2010

✓ "Boethius was successful in his argument that God rewards and punishes justly". Discuss

▸ **The question as to whether or not a good God should reward and punish**

Possible future questions

★ "A good God would never punish sinners". Discuss

Life and death

▸ **Distinctions between body and soul, as expressed in the thinking of Plato, Aristotle, John Hick and Richard Dawkins**

June 2010

✓ Critically compare Aristotle's and Richard Dawkins' views on body and soul

Possible future questions

★ Critically compare John Hick's and Plato's views on body and soul

★ Critically compare Plato's and Aristotle's views on body and soul

▸ **Other concepts of the body/soul distinction**

May 2011

✓ Evaluate the claim that the soul is distinct from the body

Possible future question

★ "The body and soul are one entity". Discuss

▸ **Different views of life after death: resurrection and reincarnation**

Jan 2011

✓ "Resurrection is more likely to be true than reincarnation". Discuss

The examiner comments about this question: It was disappointing that very

few said anything about what was needed to be a continuous person, a question which for many philosophers is central to the plausibility of either theory of life after death.

Possible future question

★ Critically evaluate the view that human beings can be reincarnated.

▸ **Questions surrounding the nature of disembodied existence**

Jan 2010

✓ Evaluate the claim that there can be no disembodied existence after death

✓ 'Life after death cannot involve a physical form". Discuss

▸ **The relationship between the afterlife and the problem of evil**

June 2010

✓ To what extent is belief in an afterlife necessary for resolving problems raised by the existence of evil

Possible future question

★ "The existence of an afterlife makes sense of an unjust world". Discuss

A2 ETHICS (OCR G582)

The A2 specification includes the theories studied in the AS syllabus. On three out of 24 questions set the examiner has specifically mentioned one of these theories: Jan 2010 (Utilitarianism linked to the environment), June 2012 (Religious Ethics and Business), and Jan 2011 (Natural Law and Sex). So we need to revise these old theories and relate them particularly to issues in business and environmental ethics, and issues in sexual ethics. In the analysis below, we examine which areas of the syllabus have been examined on up to June 2012, and the questions we might expect in the future are indicated by a star.

Ethical topics and theories: Meta-ethics

▸ **Examine how ethical language (good, bad, right, wrong) is used**

Possible future question

★ "The meaning of 'good' varies from ethical theory to ethical theory". Discuss

▸ **Explore how meta-ethics is different from normative ethics**

Possible future question

★ "Meta-ethical theories are of no practical use". Discuss

▸ **Examine the different approaches using terms such as cognitive, non-cognitive, naturalism, emotivism, prescriptivism and intuitionism.**

These then need to be applied to ethical statements

June 2011

TICK "Ethical statements are no more than expressions of emotion". Discuss

Jan 2012

✓ "All ethical language is prescriptive". Discuss

May 2012

✓ Asks us to examine the extent to which moral statements have objective meaning. (The word "objective" is not in this syllabus but occurs in theory section of the AS syllabus)

Possible future questions

★ "Ethical language is essentially naturalistic". Discuss

★ "All moral language is based on intuition". Discuss

★ Critically assess whether all moral language is subjective

▸ **Assess the different theories critically**

Jan 2010

✓ To what extent is ethical language meaningful?

Possible future question

★ Critically assess which meta-ethical theory is most useful in determining the meaning of ethical language

Ethical topics: Free will and determinism

▸ **Examine three approaches: hard determinism, soft determinism and libertarianism**

Possible future question

★ Critically assess the libertarian approach to free will and moral responsibility

▸ **Examine and understand the views of Darrow, Honderich, Hume and Locke**

Possible future question

★ Critically assess Honderich's theory of determinism

▸ **Look at religious aspects of free will and predestination**

Possible future question

★ "Free will is incompatible with predestination: therefore God cannot judge us". Discuss

▸ **Look at different influences, such as genes, psychology, environment and social conditioning for moral choices**

Jan 2011

✓ "Our ethical decisions are merely the result of social conditioning". Discuss

Possible future question

★ "Human beings are a product of genes and environment. Therefore there can be no moral responsibility". Discuss

▸ **Look at the implications of 2.4 for moral responsibility**

▸ **Examine the links between free will, determinism and moral responsibility**

June 2010

✓ Critically assess the claim that people are free to make moral choices

May 2011

✓ Critically assess the view that we are not responsible for our actions

▸ **Discuss all these elements critically**

Jan 2012

✓ Asks us to examine whether free will is compatible with determinism

Possible future question

★ "If hard determinism is true there can be no moral responsibility". Discuss

Ethical theories: Nature and role of conscience

▸ **Differentiate between the ideas of conscience as God-given, innate and produced by reason as an "inner voice", or instilled by society, parents and authority figures**

Jan 2011

✓ Critically assess whether conscience is the voice of reason

The examiner commented on students answers: "Some candidates who discussed Aquinas did not seem clear about his ideas on conscience and did not refer to synderesis, conscientia or recta ratio. There also tended to be little distinction between the views of Butler or Newman", (Jan 2011 report).

May 2012

✓ This question linked Butler's theory to the idea of Innateness

Possible future questions

★ "Conscience is a product of our upbringing and environment, and so is an unreliable authority for moral decisions". Discuss

★ Critically assess the view that conscience is the voice of God

▸ **Consider whether conscience is a reliable guide to moral decision-making**

Jan 2010

✓ Assess the view that conscience need not always be obeyed

Jan 2012

✓ Asks us to discuss whether the demands of conscience are overriding for issues surrounding sex

▸ **Consider specific views: of Augustine, Aquinas, Butler, Newman, Freud, Fromm and Piaget**

Possible future questions

★ Critically assess the view that Freudian theories of conscience undermine ideas of free will

★ Compare and evaluate the views of Fromm and Freud on the origins of conscience

Ethical topics: Virtue ethics

▸ **Examine the principles of Virtue Ethics starting with Aristotle**

Possible future question

★ "Aristotelean Virtue Ethics is superior to modern approaches". Discuss

▸ **Understand what it means to call Virtue Ethics "agent-centred"**

Possible future question

★ Critically assess agent-centred moral theories against law-based theories as a guide to practical decision-making

▸ **Understand the concepts of eudaimonia and the Golden Mean**

Possible future question

★ "The goal of eudaimonia gives the clearest basis for determining moral goodness". Discuss

▸ **Examine the importance of practising the virtues and following virtuous people**

May 2011

✓ To what extent is Virtue Ethics useful in making decisions surrounding extra-marital sex?

▸ **Compare Aristotle with more modern theories (but doesn't mention anyone specifically)**

Jan 2012

✓ To what extent does modern Virtue Ethics address the weaknesses of Aristotle's teaching on virtue?

Applied ethics: Environmental and business

▸ **Ask how we as humans should relate to the environment**

Possible future question

★ "We have a duty to protect the environment". Discuss

▸ **Understand secular approaches (the Gaia hypothesis)**

Possible future question

★ "The Gaia hypothesis is the only theory that gives moral significance to the environment". Discuss

▸ **Examine issues in business and mentions two relationships - with consumers, and employees**

Possible future question

★ "Business puts profit before people and so lacks an ethical basis for decisions". Discuss

▸ **Understand the relationship between business and the environment and business and the idea of globalisation**

Jan 2011

✓ "The environment suffers because business has no ethics". Discuss

The examiner commented on student answers: "Many gave emotive responses, writing about the importance of the environment without questioning the role of business or being able to provide any evidence for their responses", (Jan 2011 report).

Possible future question

★ "Ethical theories cannot guide business effectively in making decisions on issues surrounding globalisation". Discuss

▸ **Apply the different theories (secular and religious, including those studied at AS level) to issues raised by environmental and business ethics**

Jan 2010

✓ "Utilitarianism is not the best approach to environmental issues". Discuss

June 2010

✓ Assess the usefulness of Religious Ethics as an ethical approach to business. {Notice this is one of three occasions out of 24 questions set (2010-1012) where an ethical theory from the **AS SYLLABUS** is mentioned}

✓ A second one is the question above linking Utilitarianism to the environment

May 2012

✓ Asked a question linking business behaviour to ethical principles

May 2012

✓ Asks us to discuss whether there is a moral imperative to care for the environment. Notice this is the **ONLY TIME** two questions have been asked from one section of the syllabus.

Possible future question

★ "Ethical theories cannot take into account issues raised by the environment because no theory considers morally significant those yet unborn". Discuss

Applied ethics: Sexual ethics

▸ **Understand the issues surrounding pre-marital sex, extra-marital sex, contraception and homosexuality**

June 2010

✓ To what extent are ethical theories useful in considering issues surrounding homosexuality

Jan 2011

✓ "Natural Law is the most reliable approach when considering the issues surrounding premarital sex". Discuss

This is one of three questions out of 24 surveyed which specifically mentions an AS theory. The examiner commented on student answers: "Some candidates made good use of the phrase 'most reliable approach' and were able to posit a range of more reliable or less reliable approaches, with clear evaluation as to the reasons for these views".

Possible future questions

★ To what extent are ethical theories useful when considering issues surrounding contraception

★ To what extent are ethical theories useful in considering issues surrounding extramarital sex

★ "Virtue Ethics is the best approach to issues surrounding sex and relationships". Discuss

▸ **Review and analyse how the theories we have studied at AS level and A2 might help us apply ethical principles to the issues raised by the previous point**

Jan 2010

✓ "Some ethical theories are more useful than others in making decisions about sexual issues". Discuss {Note: you are expected to know **AS theories** plus Virtue Ethics for this question - selecting two and contrasting them might be the best approach}.

May 2011

✓ To what extent is Virtue Ethics helpful when making decisions about extra-marital sex?

Jan 2012

✓ Asks us to discuss whether the demands of conscience are overriding for issues surrounding sex

Possible future questions

★ "Ethical theories are of no practical use when considering issues raised by contraception". Discuss

★ "The morality of homosexuality is a matter of personal opinion". Discuss

What the Examiner Says

Every year the examiner produces a report on student answers available on the OCR website. It is possible to extract from these general principles what goes wrong when you write essays under exam conditions. Actually the same points are made over and over again, as if no-one ever reads the reports and if they do, fail to learn from them. I have summarised here the main points the examiner makes, and then I suggest twelve things to practise to try and eliminate these errors.

AS PHILOSOPHY AND ETHICS

Answer the question

It sounds an obvious point, but nearly every year the examiner complains that students are deviating off the question, either because you have learned a pre-prepared answer, or because you have more knowledge on another (perhaps related) area and so feel compelled to prove it.

Enormous efforts are made for little credit as this comment in January 2011 indicates:

> "*An examination at this level is not primarily a test of what candidates know, but rather of how well they can respond to the question. Some candidates wrote at enormous length, covering every theory they could remember, but often without demonstrating how these might be remotely relevant*".

As another example, here's a comment praising relevance from a recent report:

> *"Good candidates kept the question in mind throughout"*, *(Jan 2012 AS Ethics Q4b)*

You will not achieve an A grade if you don't answer the exact question set.

When you go into an exam, take a highlighter pen and highlight the key words and phrases. Hopefully, if you study this book carefully, you will understand what sort of command words (like 'Explain") to expect, and indeed, what kind of questions, as the examiner tends to repeat key phrases in different questions. A comment like the one below is fairly typical:

> *"Generally, candidates fared well provided they answered the question which had been set and not the one they hoped would be set. Candidates need to be reminded to read the question and then answer the question".* June 2012

▸ **Practise: making a reference to the question in every paragraph you write**

▸ **Know your key terms throughly**

In a previous chapter I listed the technical vocabulary in different areas of the syllabus. This creates a minimal list of technical terms you must thoroughly understand and know. There is no excuse for entering an exam in a state of muddle over the distinction between a priori and a posteriori. Here are two comments from recent examiner's reports.

> *"Words which seemed to have been ignored (or misunderstood) are 'universe', 'inconsistent' and 'biblical'," (Jan 2012 AS Philosophy) "Significant numbers seemed unaware that a predicate is part of a sentence and is not a quality of a thing". (June 2012 AS Philosophy)*

Then in a longer extract, the examiner reiterates this point:

> *"Unfortunately, there are still candidates who attempt this examination with insecure knowledge of basic philosophical concepts and terminology. Many remain unaware of the correct meaning of terms such as 'empirical', 'logical ', 'refute', 'metaphysical', 'a priori' or 'a posteriori'. Especially common errors were 'analytical' for 'analytic' – especially and 'scientifical' for 'scientific'. This subject presupposes familiarity with basic philosophical notions and some candidates have paid too little attention to these".*

‣ **Practise: learning key definitions off by heart**

‣ **Reflect, don't just memorise**

> *"Some candidates appeared to have attempted to learn theories, leading to less successful responses: more able responses showed evidence of reflection on theories, with the best showing the benefits of original thought. It cannot be too often stressed that examiners – and the nature of the subject – expect candidates to demonstrate that they have considered and*

reflected on ideas and not merely learned them". (AS Philosophy Jan 2012).

How do we "reflect on theories"? My argument in this book is that we reflect on theories by not just learning key points off by heart, but also by understanding (and being prepared to challenge) key **ASSUMPTIONS** the theory makes and reflecting carefully on the **WORLDVIEW** the theory comes out of. We then practise applying the key **PRINCIPLES** suggested by a theory to a particular issue (preferably using our own examples to ground the explanation).

▸ **Practise: reflective writing by peer group comparison and using examples of good practice on the PI website**

▸ **Show higher order skills**

> *"Despite good AO1 performance, AO2 skills were often lacking. It continues to be the characteristic of many candidates to believe that just because a number of philosophers have criticised a theory, it must be wrong, and when evaluating a question, you simply need to count the philosophers who make points on each side of the argument and see which side has more in it', (June 2012 examiners' report).*

What are these AO1 and AO2 skills? In general terms these "descriptors" as they are called can be expressed thus for AS and A2 (at A2 the whole essay is assessed according to these).

AO1: In part a. of AS questions you must select and demonstrate clearly relevant knowledge and understanding through the use of evidence, examples and correct language and terminology appropriate to Ethics and Philosophy of Religion.

For top marks (25/35 at AS, 21/35 at A2) you will need:

1. A very high level of ability to select and deploy relevant information

2. Accurate use of technical terms

3. A well-structured answer

AO2: In part b. of AS questions you must sustain a critical line of argument and justify a point of view.

For top marks (10/25 at AS, 14/35 at A2) you must:

1. Comprehend the demands of the question

2. Use a wide range of evidence

3. Show understanding and critical analysis of different viewpoints

▸ **Practise: reading the list of AO2 skills before you start your essay, and re-read after you've finished**

▸ **Argue, don't assert**

It's worth reflecting long and hard on the longer quotes from examiner's reports below:

> *"A statement of a viewpoint is not an argument, and argument by assertion is inappropriate in philosophical writing. Many responses simply presented alternative viewpoints but made no*

attempt to use these to work to their own conclusions. Candidates would benefit from thinking through the implications of the descriptors in the published levels of response used for marking – these are invaluable for explaining precisely those abilities rewarded by examiners". Jan 2012 AS Philosophy of Religion

"It is important that candidates engage with arguments: examiners seek evidence that views have been thoughtfully considered. A list of the arguments of different philosophers does not become a considered argument simply because 'however' is occasionally inserted into a narrative account". June 2012 AS Philosophy of Religion

"On occasions, some candidates, who were clearly very able, let themselves down by merely stating the views in detail and failing to deploy them as part of an overall argument". June 2012 AS Philosophy of Religion Q1a

"Some candidates struggled with the fundamental skill of constructing arguments, especially in part b) of questions".

▸ **Practise: constructing arguments using the thesis - argument - conclusion model described in my book How to Write Philosophy Essays**

▸ **Illustrate with examples**

"Good marks were awarded for candidates who were able to demonstrate control of the material as well as being able to give

examples from the biblical text to support their explanations".
June 2012 Q2a

But make sure the examples are fresh and relevant. 'Some candidates continued to use dubious examples to support their explanations and many not even ethical ones, as well as the usual 'helping an old lady to cross the road' and the 'stealing to feed a starving family'. Jan 2012 AS Ethics

▸ **Practise: finding film extracts, news examples, or incidents in novels that illustrate ethical principles. Watch new films critically**

▸ **Produce an argument, not a list**

It is worth reflecting again on what constitutes an argument. If you have difficulty knowing how to practise forming an argument, I give plenty of examples in my book "How to Write Philosophy Essays". Weaker candidates simply list points, rather than integrate them into a line of reasoning. A grade candidates argue and explain points, showing how they link to assumptions and worldviews. Here's a comment that confirms this problem:

> *"Weaker candidates tended to write as much as they knew without focusing on command words such as 'explain'. Some candidates continued to use dubious examples to support their explanations and many not even ethical ones, as well as the usual 'helping an old lady to cross the road' and the 'stealing to feed a starving family'", (June 2012 AS Ethics)*

And on Utilitarianism, there is this comment:

"Weaker responses simply described the differences (between Act and Rule Utilitarianism) without any explanation of the reasons behind them", (Jan 2012 AS Ethics Q1a).

▸ **Practise: producing argument plans which sketch out counter-arguments and objections, like the Socratic method**

▸ **Be aware of the various issues (and applications) within a topic**

The examiner stressed in the 2010 June report that "candidates must learn how to apply ethical theories to practical ethical issues. Many candidates do not know how to do so and therefore cannot access the higher marks".

"Unfortunately, many candidates seemed to have only a very basic knowledge of what genetic engineering involved. Many candidates only focused on human genetic engineering without mentioning animals or plants. Some candidates focused entirely on IVF treatment without discussing issues such as genetic selection or testing for disease, resulting in a limited viewpoint.". Jan 2012 AS Ethics Q2b

An example of an AS Ethics candidate praised highly by the examiner involves using an entirely correct, but unusual argument in answer to a question (Jan 2011 Q) on Natural Law "One candidate wrote an excellent response showing that Natural Law can be both absolute and relative". (Jan 2011 report on AS Ethics).

- Practise: working out the issues surrounding abortion etc and then applying moral theories to these issues. Try to extract principles from theories

- Find out about modern interpretations

Even when the syllabus doesn't mention them, the examiner clearly likes original, up-to-date comments about the theories set at AS. One example, which slightly surprised me because it seems to depart from the syllabus, is this comment about modern interpretations of Natural Law theory: 'Many were able to make reference to more modern forms of Natural Law theory as found in Proportionalism. Key features such as the concept of telos, eudaimonia, the Primary and Secondary Precepts, apparent and actual goods and intentions behind actions were often highlighted.' Jan 2012 AS Ethics Q4a

I was encouraged by this comment. The examiner is saying "don't read the syllabus over-narrowly". Why not use Christine Korsgaard (a modern Kantian) or Richard Hare (a twentieth century Utilitarian) to help reflect on these two theories? Here's another:

> "The best answers, of which there were few, were able to use the work of Norman Malcolm or Alvin Plantinga to critically attack Kant's work through the notion of God's unlimited nature or maximal greatness to support Anselm's claim that God is a special case, (June 2012 AS Philosophy Q1b)

If your teachers don't like this, quote the examiner's report back to them.

- Practise: finding modern scholars who represent different viewpoints on old questions or theories

- Consult the philosophicalinvestigations website for extracts listed by section

A2 PHILOSOPHY OF RELIGION AND ETHICS

Th examiner's report of 2012 expressed disappointment particularly in the A2 Philosophy of Religion answers. "The overall standard of responses was slightly disappointing. Many answers were general in nature and failed to address the specific question set. A significant number of candidates seemed to be incapable of identifying which area of the specification was being assessed. It was not always that candidates' material was completely irrelevant; rather that the relevance was not made clear. Paragraphs on new thinkers or ideas would appear in many responses suddenly and without explanation".

▸ **Lack of knowledge of key terms affects quality of answers**

The examiner's report repeatedly makes the same point at A2 as at AS, that key terms are not properly understood. For example: "A particular problem for many was inadequate grasp of the grammar of philosophy, with terms such as 'prove' used as a synonym for 'argue'. Some would say of each thinker cited that he had 'proved' his view, even when it was controversial or opposed by other alleged 'proofs'; 'refute' used to mean 'deny'; a priori often mistakenly used for 'innate'; a posteriori, 'analytic' and 'metaphysical' were commonly misunderstood. This is an examination in Philosophy of Religion, and understanding the conventions of the subject is as significant as understanding correct notation in Mathematics. Some candidates attempted, normally unsuccessfully, to answer philosophical questions with theological or scriptural assertions", (Jan 2012 A2 Philosophy of Religion).

▸ **Practise: writing full definitions of key terms on index cards and learn them**

> ▸ **Write critical analysis**

"The best answers were able to analyse the experiences critically, giving a variety of examples. Successful analysis employed good use of psychological evidence such as 'mass hysteria' to challenge whether these experiences were even veridical or plausible at best. There was good use of Feuerbach, Freud, James and Swinburne as well as awareness of modern scientific research such as the 'God helmet.' " Jan 2012 A2 Philosophy of Religion Q1

Sometimes the examiner praises high quality candidates who go way beyond the syllabus with their analysis. One example is a question on Meta-ethics in the January 2012 exam, asking whether ethical language is necessarily prescriptive: "Some very good candidates used the ideas of Mackie and Charles Pigden using error theory to argue that there are no moral facts so prescriptivism is wrong and we can only use ethical language in an agreed social contract which makes it convenient for use to prescribe certain moral actions as right and wrong", (Jan 2012 A2 Ethics Q1).

> ▸ **Practise: writing under timed conditions taking past questions (and looking at the mark schemes available on the OCR site) and then trying my possible future questions in Chapter 4**

> ▸ **Read the original sources**

Original sources are indicated in the specification. It is important to read these carefully and understand them for yourself, and not rely on textbook interpretations. One example is the radio debate between Copleston and Russell in the Philosophy of Religion specification.

> *"It was clear that few candidates had read the University Debate. Had the debate been read, many errors of understanding could have been avoided", (Jan 2012 A2 Philosophy of Religion Q4)*

▸ **Practise: extracting your own quotes from original sources, and taking notes which map the arguments**

▸ **Don't tack your evaluation on at the end**

The examiner has encouraged us to separate analysis and evaluation at AS level (part a. is always analysis and part b. evaluation) and now we are criticised for tacking evaluation on at the end. The only way to learn how to integrate the two effectively is to read good examples and then try to copy their style. This comes with practice. How to construct such essays, and the sort of language to use, is dealt with at length in my book, co-authored with Brain Poxon "How to Write Philosophy Essays" (pushmepress.com, 2012).

> *"Many candidates were able to attempt to analyse and evaluate elements within the main argument rather than tacked on as a paragraph at the end of their response", (Jan 2012 A2 Ethics)*

▸ **Practise: taking a contrary position to a philosopher's view and producing summary sheets of strengths and weaknesses of different viewpoints**

Postscript

Peter Baron read Politics, Philosophy and Economics at New College, Oxford and afterwards obtained an MLitt for a research degree in Hermeneutics at Newcastle University. He qualified as an Economics teacher in 1982, and from 2006-12 taught ethics at Wells Cathedral School in Somerset.

In 2007 he set up a philosophy and ethics community dedicated to enlarging the teaching of philosophy in schools by applying the theory of multiple intelligences to the analysis of philosophical and ethical problems. So far over 400 schools have joined the community and over 10,000 individuals use his website every month.

To join the community please register your interest by filling in your details on the form on the website. We welcome contributions and suggestions so that our community continues to flourish and expand.

www.philosophicalinvestigations.co.uk